Muriel T. Mason
& Japanese Theatre
Summer '81

Theatre Department

Brooklyn College

Professor Benito Ortolani,
Chrmn., Thtre. Dept.

Nō

The Classical Theatre
of Japan

DONALD KEENE

photographs by
KANEKO HIROSHI

KODANSHA INTERNATIONAL LTD.

Distributors:

United States: Harper & Row, Publishers, Inc.
10 East 53rd Street, New York 10022

Canada: Fitzhenry & Whiteside Limited
150 Lesmill Road, Don Mills, Ontario

Central and South America: Feffer & Simons Inc.
31 Union Square, New York, New York 10003

British Commonwealth (excluding Canada and the Far East):
TABS, 51 Weymouth Street, London W1

Europe: Boxerbooks Inc.
Limmatsrasse 111, 8031 Zurich

Australia and New Zealand: Paul Flesch & Co. Pty. Ltd.
259 Collins Street, Melbourne 3000

Thailand: Central Department Store Ltd.
306 Silom Road, Bangkok

Hong Kong and Singapore: Books for Asia Ltd.
30 Tat Chee Avenue, Kowloon; 65 Crescent Road,
Singapore 15

The Far East: Japan Publications Trading Company
P.O. Box 5030, Tokyo International, Tokyo

Published by Kodansha International Ltd., 2-12-21 Otowa,
Bunkyo-ku, Tokyo 112 and Kodansha International/USA,
Ltd., 10 East 53rd Street, New York, New York 10022 and
44 Montgomery Street, San Francisco, California 94104.
Copyright in Japan 1966 by Kodansha International Ltd.
All rights reserved. Printed in Japan.

Hardback edition, 1966   LCC 66-25756
Revised paperback edition, 1973   ISBN 0-87011-192-2
Second printing, 1974   JBC 3074-783745-2361

The text
is dedicated to
Naru *and* Alan Hovhaness

CONTENTS

INTRODUCTION

THE word *nō* means talent and, by extension, the display of talent in a performance. In its earliest forms Nō, an art that today enjoys enormous prestige, may have been little more than a display of acrobatics and circus stunts, but in the course of time the original Nō developed into an aristocratic, almost ritual, art. The remoteness of its style and content from the typical dramatic forms of our own day has often led prophets to declare that Nō could not long survive, that a younger generation accustomed to the pace of films and television could never tolerate the extreme deliberation of Nō. Prophets of doom always sound more authoritative than optimists, but fortunately, they are as often mistaken. Contrary to all the predictions made to me in 1953, when I first saw Nō performed, Nō thrives today as never before, and the audiences consist increasingly of young people, perhaps driven to Nō by dissatisfaction with entertainments supposedly devised for their pleasure.

Nō has often been compared to the Greek drama. The use in both of masks, a chorus, song and stately dances, and poetry of an elevated nature provides some basis for comparison. But there are important differences too. Dramas intended for the huge audiences that filled the Grecian amphitheatres could not help but differ from those intended for a small group of aristocrats at the Japanese court. More important, the conception of drama differed basically. The Greeks, in Aristotle's words, believed that a play must have a beginning, a middle and an end; but the Nō plays tend to be all end, though divided into sections of different musical tempi. The Greek dramas often conclude with the warning that we must not call a man happy until he is dead, even though at the outset of the play the hero seemed to be enjoying great good fortune; but the protagonist of a Nō play has usually died before the play begins, and the end, instead of a warning, is likely to be a promise of deliverance from the tortures he is suffering when he first appears. The Greeks built plays around characters who, though larger than ourselves and confronted by problems far more terrible than any we are likely to face, are recognizably like us; the characters in the Nō plays are hardly more than beautiful shadows, the momentary embodiments of great emotions.

The Greek and Nō dramas, then, are essentially different despite surface resemblances. They are most alike, perhaps, in retaining their appeal to audiences separated by many centuries and infinite numbers of social changes from the periods when the plays were created. Though both dramas were products of particular societies and drew from their myths, their grandeur and lofty disregard of the quotidian enables them to soar eternally. That is why they move audiences today as much as when first performed.

A person equipped with nothing more than a general sensitivity to different forms of art may be deeply moved upon his first visit to a Nō theatre. Yet I believe it is also true that the more one knows about a theatre with traditions as deep-rooted as those of Nō, the greater one's pleasure.

I have written this book in the hope of passing on to others the information I have found helpful in the enjoyment of Nō.

Photographs, it hardly needs saying, are indispensable in any study of a theatrical art, particularly one as unfamiliar in the West as Nō. I have been exceptionally fortunate in my collaborator, Mr. Kaneko Hiroshi. The patience and energy—and skill, of course—demanded by his photographs were never begrudged. Nō is perhaps the most difficult form of theatre to photograph. Long intervals pass virtually without motion onstage, to be succeeded by brief and violent action. The photographer seldom has a second chance if he misses the first time. A Nō play is performed in the season with which it is associated, and often but a single time. If the photographer misses, for example, the moment in *Tsuchigumo* when the monstrous spider throws out his web, he may have to wait a whole year before it is staged again, and it may not be staged by the same group of actors for many years. Again, the photographer who is asked for a picture of Nō being performed at the Itsukushima Shrine at a time when the stage is surrounded by water has a total of about one hour in the course of an entire year. The photographing of the masks, however, poses the greatest problems. They are prized for their ability to shift expression, and the photographer therefore bears the responsibility, through his choice of lighting and angle, for the face that each mask presents to the world.

A problem encountered by anyone preparing an illustrated book on Nō arises from the difficulty of obtaining permission to examine the masks and costumes of the different schools. Mr. Maruoka Akira made it possible to obtain the cooperation of the leading actors; I owe him especial thanks.

I have failed thus far to mention the Kyōgen farces which are equally the subject of this book. This does not reflect any lack of esteem. Indeed, I believe my happiest experiences in Japan were studying and performing in Kyōgen for several years. But Kyōgen is altogether a more genial and outgoing art than Nō and requires little introduction here. I wish, however, to express my thanks to the artists of both Ōkura and Izumi schools for their kind cooperation.

Finally, I must thank the staff of Kodansha International Ltd. for having contrived to satisfy my every request for this book, however unreasonable. Requests for photographs that most publishers in other countries would have refused even to consider—for the costumes of the Kongō school in Kyoto, displayed only at the height of the sweltering summer, or for the rustic versions of Nō performed at Kurokawa in the depths of the bitter northern winter—were cheerfully met and the generosity shown me was a source of real inspiration.

DONALD KEENE

Nō

The conventional way of describing Japanese pronunciation, as rendered in roman letters, is to say that the consonants are as in English, the vowels as in Italian or Spanish. This formula is inexact, but at least it suggests the original pronunciations. All vowels are sounded; thus, the word *kakegoe* is pronounced something like *kah-keh-go-eh*, each syllable being given equal stress.

I have used the transcription Nō to designate the art, though Noh is also familiar.

Throughout the book, Japanese names retain their original order, with family name first and given or adopted name last.

I. THE PLEASURES OF NŌ

Nō BEGINS with a mask, and within the mask the presence of a god. Before a performance of *Okina*, the mask to be worn is displayed in the dressing room and honored with ritual salutations. When the actors have filed onto the stage and taken their places, one called the Mask Bearer offers the mask of *Okina* to another, who prostrates himself in reverence before accepting it. The *Okina* mask is unlike that for any other role; though its features are those of a benevolent old man and not a fearsome being, they are nonetheless a god's, and performing this role, devoid though it is of emotion or special displays of technique, is considered so arduous as to shorten the life of the actor.

Okina, the oldest Nō play, is accorded unusual reverence, but even plays not about the gods partake of the mystery of divinity. Before the actor makes his entrance he gazes at his masked face in the mirror, and though until that moment an ordinary man—whether an outcaste or a nobleman—he himself becomes as he stares at the mask a reflection. Other theatres are often said to be a mirror of life, but Nō is an image in the mirror which life approximates.

The wall at the back of the Nō stage (the *kagami-ita*, or "mirror boards") is decorated with the painting of a huge pine, the Yōgō Pine at the Kasuga Shrine in Nara. Old accounts tell how once an old man was seen performing a dance beneath this pine; he proved to be the god of the shrine. Every year, at the festival of the shrine, the head of the Komparu school of Nō stands beneath the Yōgō Pine so that the god may descend into the actor and make him his reflection. Originally, perhaps, the play merely allowed the god to assume visible form. *Okina* opens with the meaningless but portentous syllables of the god's utterance: the actor, like a medium, pronounces a language he himself cannot comprehend. *Okina* is not in the least tragic. It is a joyous celebration of abundance and long life, but the presence of the god exhausts the actor. Of all Nō plays, *Okina* is probably the most widely performed. At the beginning of the year, on important occasions, at village festivals, *Okina* normally opens the program. It has no plot, is largely unintelligible to the audience, and has little in common with popular stage entertainments, but no one would dream of omitting it; *Okina* is an initiation into the world of Nō.

The solemnity of Nō distinguishes it most conspicuously from other theatres. The Japanese are by no means incapable of comedy. Indeed, interspersed between the Nō tragedies during a complete program are farces called Kyōgen which are filled with humor. The mask of *Okina* itself, a cheerful face, has suggested to some Japanese critics that originally it was a festive work, rather than the stately ceremonial of today. For that matter, the origin of all varieties of Japanese theatre is sometimes traced to the lewd and comic dance performed by the goddess Uzume to lure the sun goddess from the cave where she sulked. But whatever the ancient manner of presentation may have been, a felicitous Nō is today performed with the deliberation and gravity reserved in most parts of the world for sacred rites. The plays are almost all tragic, but even on the rare occasion when the actor says, "How happy I am!" (*Ureshi ya!*) he sounds to the uninitiated spectator like a tortured soul.

The plays were certainly not always acted before spectators wrapped in the hushed awe of a present-day Tokyo audience. Nō performances in rural districts are sometimes as informal as the theatre in China or Southeast Asia. People chatter, eat or doze through the performance, and no one takes it amiss if a well-wisher, sympathizing with the actors on a cold night, steps onto the stage to offer them hot saké. This may have been the normal reception of the Nō plays before court patronage in the fourteenth century gave them an aristocratic dignity. The ritualization of Nō in the seventeenth century imparted to the theatre its present solemnity.

But even if Nō was once lighter entertainment, the plays were performed in a building belonging to a shrine, and the actors, then as today, were participants in a rite. The religion served by the performers is Shinto, the Way of the Gods. This native religion of Japan has its sacred book and a body of theological writings, but most Japanese believe in Shinto not in terms of its formal mythology and the scholars' elucidations, but in terms of gods and demons inhabiting the mountains and waters of Japan. These supernatural beings are innumerable, and include emperors, the ghosts of famous men, animals, trees, and even inanimate objects. The good spirits bring happiness and plenty, but there are also malevolent ghosts. One way to appease the dead, who might otherwise return to afflict the living, was to recite or re-enact their deeds on earth, assuring them that they had not been forgotten. The sacred dances at the Shinto shrine, Kagura, originated in this manner, it appears, and Nō may also have been intended to calm the troubled dead. The dead return to life on the Nō stage to tell again their hours of glory and grief.

We cannot be sure how Nō came to assume its present form or what its relation was to religious rituals. Often we must guess from a survival in some remote village, an older form of Nō than the more polished art in the cities. Sometimes too we can obtain hints by examining the theatre elsewhere. In Thailand, for example, plays are performed today on a row of tiny stages before the great stupa at Nakhorn Pathom—not for an audience (though a few old people and children may be present), but for the gods. The family of a recently deceased person offers the plays, which are staged with the utmost intensity, even without an audience. Perhaps this was true in Japan in ancient times. Nō stages have three steps leading down from the front. These have no function in performances (though, one may be wryly informed, an actor who fell from the stage could use them to climb back). In the past the actors were rewarded after a performance with gifts from the daimyo they served, presented by an official who used the steps for the purpose. But originally, perhaps, the steps were added so that the actors, priests at a Shinto shrine, might pass from the shrine to the stage where they performed not for an audience of mortals but for the gods.

Today, a performance of Nō, like any other theatrical representation, demands not only a stage and actors but an audience, and its purpose is to provide "entertainment." However, the stage, actors, and audience differ so markedly from those in theatres elsewhere that we are apt to be less conscious of what Nō shares with drama in other countries (or with other forms of drama within Japan itself) than of its uniqueness. The entertainment it provides is unlikely to afford a casual visitor much distraction, but it possesses immediately recognizable beauty: the masks, superb examples of the carver's art; the magnificent costumes; the hypnotically eloquent singing of the chorus; the stately movements of the actors. Yet as soon as one enters a Nō theatre one realizes from the austere stage, the respectful hush of the audience, that it is the scene not merely of drama but of ritual. An appreciation of the ritual of Nō may come intuitively and instantly, as Western visitors sometimes discover, or it may be the product of years of study. Nō gives pleasure in proportion to what the spectators bring to their appreciation, whether a sensitivity to any form of beauty, or a specific knowledge of the texts, movement and music. Because Nō makes no concessions, the slowness of pace and unrelieved gravity may weary, but this risk is taken deliberately.

The purpose of Nō is not to divert on the surface but to move profoundly and ultimately, to transcend the particular and touch the very springs of human emotions.

Of all theatres probably Nō makes the greatest demands on the audience. The texts are in medieval language, studded with quotations from even older classics, and would be difficult to follow even if pronounced with the utmost clarity. The actors scorn as mere "theatricality" any suggestion of realism in representation, and the audience is prepared to accept in the role of a beautiful girl a tottering old man with a quavering voice and heavy jowls visible around the mask. A child may perform as a warrior capable of inspiring terror in demons, and no one in the audience laughs at his high-pitched little voice when he reassures his frightened followers that they have nothing to fear. The masks make it possible to believe that an actor with an unattractive face is a god or a beautiful woman; in this sense they provide a realistic touch, but the unvarying expression on Shizuka's face, whether angry, weeping, or resigned to her fate, must be given shades of meaning by the eye of the connoisseur. The appeal of Nō is by no means entirely intellectual or aesthetic; it moves many in the audience to tears, and leaves haunting and poignant remembrances.

A recent critic, reviewing the performance of a sixty-four-year-old actor in the part of Lady Rokujō in *Nonomiya* ("The Shrine in the Fields"), a play based on *The Tale of Genji* and describing the beautiful, elegant princess who desperately loved Genji, wrote, "I have never seen such a deeply-felt performance of *Nonomiya*. . . . The actor succeeded in leaving so profound and penetrating an impression that for awhile afterwards I was quite overcome, and even now I feel something like a lump in the pit of my stomach. It goes without saying that the play produced a different effect than a reading of *The Tale of Genji*, but even in terms of Nō the impression I received was at times different from any other representation I have witnessed. On this occasion Rokujō of course was beautiful, but one was made to think less of the aristocratic dignity of the woman than of her fate. Above all, I was impressed by the strength in Nō itself and in the actor's art to move men's hearts."

This performance of *Nonomiya*, by an actor whose normal appearance and voice in no way suggested a beautiful court lady, was more deeply affecting than a more realistic representation could have been. The text of *Nonomiya* is a masterpiece, but no one by reading the text alone could sense the shattering loneliness of the moment on the stage when Rokujō, standing before the *torii* of the Shrine in the Fields, lifts her foot to step through, a gesture of symbolic renunciation of the world and Prince Genji, only to return her foot to its place, yielding to a final burst of longing. The performance of the actor as Rokujō must reach its climax at this moment, and he is abetted by the harsh, desolate beat of the hand drum (*ōtsuzumi*). The actor must not only transcend his physical limitations but convert them into the elements of a supreme artistic experience. The particular qualities of an actress in the part of Rokujō might obscure the eternal, absolute nature of the princess and her tragic love, but an old man's voice, his movements perfected during half a century on the stage, the stylized beauty of his mask, costume and fan, can emphasize the eternal lines of the story. Additional realism would be as foolish as coloring in the lines of Euclid's propositions, or in as bad taste as the rubies and emeralds with which the barbarous sultans adorned their Chinese porcelains.

It has taken some six hundred years for Nō to achieve its present refinement. We have no way of telling whether actors of former days were more or less capable than those today, but the natural human tendency to glorify the past has induced critics at all times to assert that the performers of their day were no match for those of the past. Zeami (1363–1443), the greatest figure in the history of Nō, was sure that no contemporary actor could remotely touch the abilities of his father, and a writer describing performances he had seen in 1658 declared, "Nō in the old days used to encourage virtue by representing the good and chastise vice by representing the bad, and the movements of the actor's feet and head were never at variance with decorum, but modern performances, in complete violation of the old traditions, have reduced the art to vulgarity."

Each age had brought changes to the performing techniques, generally as a reflection of changing times and tastes rather than of a decline in the actors' skill. Today, at a time when other Japanese traditional arts have lost their popular following, new stages have been built for Nō, and hundreds of thousands of amateurs are learning the singing and dancing. Numbers alone do not prove that Nō is now enjoying its period of greatest distinction, but the size of the audiences means that Nō does not survive merely in a fossilized form, revived rarely and piously on special occasions like the European miracle plays. Though confined to a repertory largely established four hundred years ago, and staged in exact conformance to the traditions of the different schools of performers, Nō is a living art, changing subtly but surely with the times, as interpreted by its outstanding performers.

The Nō repertory comprises a great variety of works, ranging from virtually static celebrations of the glories of a particular shrine to pieces of violent movement in which devils assert their terrible powers. It includes works which are almost purely poetic and symbolic, suggesting the loveliness of plum blossoms or the snow, and others which treat betrayal and vengeance. Usually when critics make generalizations about Nō they are thinking of the poetic dramas associated with the name of Zeami; these plays indeed are closest to the essence of Nō. Many earlier or later pieces show a more pronounced dramatic quality and realism. They form an essential part of the repertory and, on the whole, enjoy even greater popularity than Zeami's masterpieces, but it is not for their sake that the audience goes to the Nō theatre. Though the members of the audience may prefer the stirring *Funa Benkei* ("Benkei in the Boat") to the remote loveliness of *Kakitsubata* ("The Iris"), the slow-moving, poetic works give Nō its meaning and ultimate appeal. Modern audiences, no less than their predecessors, are there to witness a special form of drama, and they respect its demands. They may be less inclined than those of fifty or more years ago to sit through a full program of plays, but they are moved by precisely the same moments: when Rokujō hesitates before the *torii*, or when the ghost of Matsukaze, the fisher girl deserted by a nobleman, disappears for the last time, "leaving only the wind in the pines." The Nō plays are admired because they capture in words, music and dance the tragic climaxes of profound emotions.

Actors today may interpret the parts with greater psychological subtlety than their predecessors, but this is not a violation of the texts, which contain poetic truth of eternal and universal validity, leaving them open to interpretation and appreciation by men of different ages and societies. Every gesture in Nō has centuries of tradition behind it, but the actor has greater leeway in interpreting the roles than in works of more specific content tied to this time or that place. Nō is realistic in its evocations of what a woman experiences when deserted by her lover or what the taste of defeat is to a hitherto unvanquished warrior. This realism, as contrasted with the fantasies of other forms of Japanese theatre, is the glory of Nō. It is found at its intensest in the slow-moving masterpieces of Zeami.

The audience at a Nō performance today consists mainly of connoisseurs. Many have learned the parts as amateurs or have seen performances so frequently they can detect the seemingly slight differences that distinguish a great actor from a merely competent one. Some carry texts of the plays to the theatre and consult them, not in the casual manner of the operagoer skimming through a libretto during the intermissions, but with minute care, noting variations in the performance from the musical notations in the printed text. Some are so engrossed by the musical aspects of the plays that they hardly lift their eyes to the stage, as if the acting were only incidental to their enjoyment. Others watch each gesture raptly, and study the shifting light and shadows on the masks or the details of the costumes. The printed texts are necessary for those who have not studied them in advance, because the deliberately muffled delivery, accentuated by the masks, makes it virtually impossible to understand the lines spoken or sung. Some in the audience, including connoisseurs, doze through whole sections of the plays, awakening instinctively for the climactic moments. The manner of enjoying the performance may differ, but each spectator has shared in the beauty of an art evolved by many men's efforts over the centuries.

Nō, created in the fourteenth century, reached its full growth by the middle of the fifteenth century. It shares much with other forms of expression during the period: it is bare, yet evocative, like the monochrome landscapes; beautiful, yet austere, like the temple gardens; preoccupied with death and the ultimate means of deliverance from life like the literary works inspired by the Buddhism of the time. The movements of the actors owe much to the martial arts that thrived in an age of warfare and to the decorum expected of the Zen priest. The actors' distinctive walk, a bare lifting of the feet from the floor, occurs also in the tea ceremony, another art perfected in the fifteenth century. These arts are all marked by an economy of means used to achieve a maximum effect, a preference for suggestion rather than representation. The Nō plays are staged before the unvarying backdrop of the Yōgō Pine, and in place of the realistic props found in some Western theatres (fountains with real water, doors that slam with a convincing bang), the props for Nō are seldom more than outlines of the objects suggested—a boat, a hut or a carriage. The gestures of the actors are highly stylized: either simplified, as when a hand lifted before the slightly lowered mask denotes weeping, or developed into the pattern of a dance, as when the simple action of noticing something is depicted by the actor's bringing together his opened fan in his right hand to his left hand, slowly lifting the fan diagonally upwards, then lowering his left hand diagonally to the left as his gaze falls on an object. Above all, the masks, by eliminating not only particularities of features but any readily apparent change in emotions, evoke more in the connoisseur than the most expressive actor's face.

Suggestion, achieved through the most restrained means, is not an end in itself; like every aspect of Nō it is intended to achieve beauty. Nō is a supremely aesthetic theatre. Critics and commentators from the time of Zeami have devoted their greatest attention to beauty of effects rather than, say, how an audience can be moved to tears. A Nō play must move the audience, but never by ugliness or violence. The humblest character—a fisher girl or a peasant—wears magnificent robes and speaks great poetry. But even beauty is not the final object. Nō reaches out towards eternity through beauty and the elimination of the temporal and accidental.

The Nō plays are set in the distant past and no attempt is made to give them immediacy. The characters are sometimes historical, sometimes drawn from the fiction of the tenth and eleventh centuries, sometimes the gods of legends, but the subjects and their treatment are so absolute that it is irrelevant to ask whether or not the plays are faithful to the times they portray. The performances too are absolute. The actor's vocal delivery and walk are identical whether he is taking the part of a man or a woman; gestures which might indicate the age or sex of the character are avoided in most plays, and the choice of masks and costumes is governed largely by tradition. Above all, the actor refrains from admixing anything of his own personality in the roles and from allowing any variation to creep into successive performances. Hōshō Kurō (1837–1917), the creator of modern Nō, said that the difference between an amateur and a professional Nō actor was that the professional always played a part in exactly the same manner. The characters depicted in the plays, however vividly they may emerge through the poetry and the movements, exist only as part of the play; it would be absurd to wonder what they were like when younger or in happier circumstances. Their absoluteness makes the plays as valid today as when written; it may be that performances are now closer to the authors' intent than was possible when the whims of courtiers might disrupt a program. In any case, despite their heavy reliance on classical poetry and unfamiliar Buddhist thought, they are immediately affecting both to Japanese and Western spectators, and can be accepted unconditionally by readers capable of enjoying poetry and myth. The powerful effect produced on Yeats and Pound, though they never saw a play performed, suggests the universality of the appeal of the Nō plays as literature.

The plays, indeed, are among the supreme masterpieces of Japanese literature, combining a richness of language and an integrity of emotion. They are so filled with ambiguities, allusions and wordplays that it seems hardly possible their first audiences could catch more than the general drift of many passages, yet they definitely were not armchair dramas. For Zeami the plays were chiefly vehicles for the display of the singing and dancing of the actors. In Europe the great plays, whether or not performed, have been read and esteemed as literature, but in Japan the evaluation of the plays has been intimately connected with performance; unstaged plays have aroused no interest. Paradoxically, the Nō is absolutely dependent on the beauty of its texts, for the deliberate manner of delivering the lines tends to exaggerate their qualities. Of the thousands of Nō plays written during the last six centuries (many, of course, intended for performance on a single occasion only), only some 230 survive in the repertory. Some have retained their popularity despite weaknesses in the text, thanks to the beauty of the music or the dances, but the vast majority are works of literary distinction.

If we attempt to examine the Nō plays in terms of some traditional definitions of drama in the West, we become immediately aware of how unsuited these criteria are. Drama begins with conflict, we are often told, but scholars of Nō have insisted that the Nō plays totally lack conflict because there is only one true personage, the *shite*, or protagonist; the other persons are merely observers of the action and not antagonists. The point is overstated, but it contains truth; most Nō plays lack the confrontation of characters typical of drama elsewhere, and some are virtually devoid of action. *Yōrō* ("Nurturing the Aged") tells of the discovery of a mineral spring with miraculous curative powers, a happy augury for the emperor's reign. The story is felicitous, but hardly dramatic. *Unrin-in*, as currently performed, is concerned mainly with explaining the meaning of certain obscure poetical terms in the tenth-century novel *Ise Monogatari*. Numerous other plays are mainly retellings of the history of a shrine or some other auspicious site, described with no suggestion of conflict.

Another Western view of drama, which stresses the importance of the creation of characters, reached its absurd heights with such nineteenth-century studies as *The Girlhoods of Shakespeare's Heroines*. But even though the *shite* is the only personage in a Nō play, he possesses few individual qualities. More often he is the incarnation of some powerful emotion, whether unforgiving enmity, possessive jealousy, or remorse for some unspeakable deed. In the early plays, before Zeami imprinted Nō with his view of the art, and in the late plays written as the form was disintegrating, more distinctive personalities are depicted, and sometimes there is conflict between the *shite* and another character. Normally, however, the *waki* ("person at the side") is little more than a representative of the audience who asks the questions it might ask, not possessing a personality or even a name of his own. The *shite* may have one or more *tsure* ("companion"), but the *tsure* is usually no more than a shadow. The *shite*, then, is generally the only person in a play, but even the *shite* belongs to another world, not our own, and creation of character, in the sense that the term is used in other forms of drama, is meaningless in Nō.

Some students of Nō, calling attention to the prominence of the final dance *(shimai)* performed by the *shite*, which may occupy a third of the total time of the play, have considered Nō as a form of spectacle and the texts as the means of creating the circumstances and atmosphere necessary for the dance. Certainly Zeami devoted enormous care to the choreography of the plays, and our most lasting impression of such a work as *Hagoromo* ("The Feather Cloak") is of the unearthly final dance of the angel. But some Nō plays are without dancing or are provided with only the suggestion of a final dance. Many are virtually without movement. Indeed, the less movement in a play, the higher its "rank" *(kurai)*. *Sekidera Komachi*, a work of so lofty a rank that in the past century only half-a-dozen actors, all acclaimed masters at the close of their careers, have ventured to perform the role, lasts about two hours; during the first hour and a half the *shite* sits motionless inside the prop, a frame representing a thatch-covered hut. A critic who saw the performance in

1955 reported that the interest of the play was mainly in the motionless hour and a half. Zeami himself wrote that the moments without action were especially appreciated by the audience; the actor, unable to rely on movement or words to distract the audience, had somehow to communicate his underlying spiritual strength. The final dance is extremely important to Nō, and may make reading the plays seem only a shell of the whole work, but the dance itself is not so much a display of agility or brilliance of movement as a continuation in different idiom of the mood created by the motionlessness.

It might be imagined, finally, that Nō resembled opera in being a drama which exists primarily for the sake of music. The music is unquestionably a vital part of Nō. The music and words have always been inseparable, the texts being transmitted orally, each syllable sung or declaimed in accordance with the musical traditions of a school of Nō. But no one ever sang the music without the words, as often happens with opera. Nor do the dances exist apart from the words in which they are framed. The music, played by drums and a flute, or sung, and the dances at the end or elsewhere, spring from the words and are in essence one with them.

A Nō play, then, fits badly into any category established by conventional Western theories of drama. To attempt a definition: it is a dramatic poem concerned with remote or supernatural events, performed by a dancer, often masked, who shares with lesser personages and a chorus the singing and declamation of the poetry. The texts of Nō are most properly discussed as literature, as in Chapter III.

Nō can be performed on any kind of stage, whether a hastily revamped modern auditorium stage or the crude platform built for a village festival, but to be appreciated fully it should be seen in a theatre built for its special use. Some old stages survive, such as the one at the shrine at Miyajima on the Inland Sea, where at certain times of day the tide flows between the audience and the stage, heightening the sense of mysterious distance. At the Nishi Honganji in Kyoto one can sit in splendor like the barons of former days, surrounded by sliding screens covered in gold leaf, and watch from a separate building the performance on the old stage. Between the seats of the nobles and the stage is a gravel-covered area where in former days the "groundlings" sat. In all Nō theatres today the tradition of having the stage in a building separate from the audience is vestigially retained by a massive wooden roof over the stage, even in modern concrete theatres. Though the gravelled area has shrunk to a symbolic foot or so, it too continues to divide the world of the audience from that of the actors.

The audience sits on two sides of the stage, to the center and to stage-right. Most Nō theatres today have seats like those in a Western theatre, but the ground floor of the older ones is divided into boxes where four or five people can sit in Japanese style, warming their hands over a *hibachi* in winter, or perhaps eating lunch from tiered lacquer boxes. The stage itself, some eighteen feet square, is built of polished but unpainted *hinoki* wood. At each of its four corners are pillars supporting the heavy curved roof. Behind the stage proper is an addition about nine feet deep (*atoza*) where the musicians and stage assistants sit; it is distinguished from the main stage by the horizontal direction of the floor boards. To stage-left is another extension, a mere three feet wide, where the chorus sits in two rows. The boards here run parallel to those of the stage. A passageway called the *hashigakari*, of the same width as the *atoza*, leads to the stage from the backstage. The *hashigakari* ranges in length from eighteen to forty-five feet, depending on the size of the theatre. On the side closer to the audience three small living pines are planted at regular intervals. At the far end is a brocade curtain with vertical stripes of contrasting colors which is lifted to permit actors to make their entrance. Two other architectural features are a low door (*kirido*) to the left of the *atoza* and the three steps leading from the stage to the gravel. Underneath the stage, invisible to the audience, are large jars placed to increase the resonance of the actors' voices and the musical instruments.

The beginning of a play is signalled from offstage by a flute. The Nō flute has not the softly melodic quality of the European flute, but sounds shrill and sometimes harsh. Its notes at the start of a performance seem to come from another world, not the Elysian Fields of the celebrated flute solo from Gluck's *Orfeo ed Eurydice* but a world infinitely distant from ours filled with a suffering we cannot comprehend. After the flute has sounded, the brocade curtain is lifted by men holding bamboo poles inserted in the hems, and the musicians enter, gravely walking in single file along the edge of the *hashigakari*, as if unwilling to tread the same boards in the center over which the actors presently will appear. The members of the chorus, eight or ten men, enter at the same time from the *kirido* at stage-left and take their places, sitting in formal Japanese style, their fans on the floor before them. The musicians sit in a prescribed order: the flutist, on the floor, farthest to stage-left; next, the player of the small drum (*kotsuzumi*) on a folding stool; the *ōtsuzumi* drummer, also on a stool; and finally, (in many but not all plays) the bass drum (*taiko*) player, kneeling on the stage a little to the rear of the others. Stage understudies (*kōken*), attired in formal black kimonos, sit at the rear of the stage, rising occasionally during the course of performance to straighten an actor's robe. The *kōken* is normally a distinguished performer capable of taking over from the *shite* if he becomes indisposed or to prompt if an actor forgets his lines.

When the musicians are seated, the flutist again plays, this time joined by the percussion instruments—the hollow thud of the *kotsuzumi* and the sharp crack of the *ōtsuzumi*. These sounds are augmented by the inarticulate, portentous cries of the drummers, suggesting again the immense distance separating the audience from the persons in the play. The brocade curtain, lowered after the musicians had all appeared, is again lifted, this time to permit the entrance of an actor and the beginning of the play.

The roles in a Nō play are known not by the names of the characters, as in a Western drama, but by the category of the role. In addition to the *shite*, *waki*, and *tsure* mentioned above, there are *kokata* (child parts, a variety of *tsure*) and *kyōgen*, generally rustics or menials. In the late Nō plays these distinctions often seem arbitrary. In some, the *waki* is more important than the *shite*, and in a few it is not even clear which part is *shite* and which *waki*. But in the plays of the great period, the first half of the fifteenth century, the *shite* is of predominant importance. The distinction between *shite* and *waki* is heightened in performance by the marked difference in costume (the *shite* wears brocades, the *waki* usually the black robes of a priest); in the use of masks for the *shite*, but never for the *waki*; in the different quality of the singing and recitation; and in the dances, which give the role of the *shite* its authority even if the part has less dialogue than the *waki*'s.

Many plays open with the entrance of the *waki*, often an itinerant monk, who tells us he intends to visit a certain shrine. His walk is deliberate, and his facial expression grave. He may describe his journey, but it is suggested in performance merely by a few steps. Eventually, he goes to the pillar at front stage-left, known as the *waki* pillar, and there awaits the appearance of the *shite*.

Nō plays are in either one scene or two. The difference is not merely in setting or length, but depends also on the nature of the play—whether about a ghost or a more realistic work. Most plays in one scene are about persons who belong to this world. The *shite*, if taking the part of a male character of his own age, may appear without a mask. In plays in two scenes, however, the *shite*'s appearance changes in the second part, and he may even be an entirely different person. In *Atsumori* we see the *shite* in the first scene as a humble reaper, but after the interlude he reappears in the second scene wearing the splendid armor of a general, his "true" appearance; this time, if not before, he wears a mask. In *Funa Benkei*, the *shite* in the first part is the unhappy Shizuka, a beautiful woman whose lover, Yoshitsune, must leave her behind as he sets out on a dangerous journey; in the second scene the *shite* is the terrible, vengeful spirit of Tomomori, a warrior vanquished by Yoshitsune, who rises from the sea to menace his ship. In this case, naturally, every detail of the *shite*'s appearance will be different in the second scene. The *tsure* accompanying the *shite* may also change appearance, but the *waki*, who belongs to this world, remains the same throughout whether in plays of one or two scenes.

The *kokata* performers appear not only in the roles of children, but also as fully-grown emperors, perhaps to avoid any suggestion of disrespect, and in most plays where an inappropriate romantic element might be created if fully grown actors appeared as man and woman in the *shite* and *tsure* parts. Yoshitsune in *Funa Benkei* is played by a boy, but in *Shōzon* a boy takes Shizuka's part. *Kokata*, whether they appear as males or females, are never masked.

The chorus, eight or ten men dressed in matching formal kimonos, sits at the side of the stage throughout the play, taking no part in the action. The function of the chorus is to recite for the actors, particularly when they are dancing. Unlike the chorus in a Greek play, it makes no comment on the action, and is never identified as townsmen, warriors or demons; the chorus, in fact, has no identity, but exists solely as another voice for the actors. Any *shite* actor, from the head of the school down, may appear in the chorus, remaining anonymous in the ranks.

The *kyōgen* parts are taken by actors attired in conspicuously humbler costumes than even the *waki*'s sombre robes. In the two-scene plays they appear during the interlude *(ai)*, generally as a rustic or "a man of the place," who explains to the *waki* the history of some remarkable occurrence. The interval *kyōgen* recitations possess slight interest for modern day spectators, who often go out for a smoke when the performer appears, but originally, when the texts were not yet printed nor so carefully studied, the *ai-kyōgen* actor was probably welcomed by the audience because he explained in a more colloquial, though eloquent, language the story so cryptically related elsewhere in the play. Perhaps also *ai-kyōgen* satisfied a craving for rhetoric, for occasions did not exist for oratory in the days when Nō was created. Today, the *ai-kyōgen*'s chief importance is that it fills the stage while the *shite* is changing costume, though a few are display pieces of narration or have an intrinsic dramatic interest.

In contrast to the *ai-kyōgen*, which rarely are humorous and are considered of such slight literary interest that they are usually omitted from texts of the plays, the independent Kyōgen, presented in alternation with the Nō plays as part of the program, are enjoyed as comedies, the best Japanese literature provides. Kyōgen farces seem to have supplied the necessary compensating humor to the unrelieved tragedy of the Nō plays from the inception of this form of theatre. Kyōgen may even be older than Nō; Kyōgen actors figure prominently in performances of *Okina*. An account of 1464 indicates that Nō and Kyōgen regularly alternated by that time if not much earlier. Although denied the prestige of Nō, Kyōgen has long shared its stage and some of its glory.

A single Nō play now takes from one to two hours to perform, depending chiefly on the length of the dances; even the most extended texts rarely run to ten pages of print. In the past the plays were performed much more quickly than today, perhaps at twice the speed, as we can judge from the number of plays presented as part of a single day's program. One play, however perfect, was never considered sufficient entertainment, and it was the practice instead to perform a series of plays in a prescribed order of categories. *Okina* was set apart, no doubt because it clearly belonged to an older tradition than the rest, and was invariably performed at the start of a program. The other plays of the repertory were divided into five categories: (1) plays about the gods *(waki Nō)*; (2) plays about martial heroes *(shuramono)*; (3) plays about women *(kazuramono)*; (4) plays of a miscellaneous or contemporary character *(genzaimono)*; and (5) plays about demons *(kiri Nō)*. The order of these five categories was determined primarily by their prevailing tempo. Each play was considered to consist of three main sections: *jo*, the introduction; *ha*, the development; and *kyū*, the climax. The pace of the play gradually increases in tempo from the deliberate introduction to the strenuous and sometimes agitated movements of the final dance. A program of Nō plays followed the same pattern. Plays of the first category, though possessing *jo*, *ha* and *kyū* sections, on the whole are slow-moving; their fastest sections are only relatively fast, and can by no means by compared to the *kyū* episodes of plays in the fourth or fifth categories. Plays of the second, third and fourth categories were considered to correspond to the *ha* section, increasing within this category from the generally slower tempo of the plays about warriors to some plays in the fourth category which depict demons in a manner almost indistinguishable from the fifth category, the *kyū* section of the program. The progression of plays was intended to provide the audience with a complete theatrical experience, starting with the stately movements of a religiously-inspired piece about the gods, a suitably elevated opening of the program, gradually increasing in human interest through the warrior play until the woman play, the most lyrical part of the program, was reached. The intensity of the woman's love portrayed in these plays might be pushed to the extreme of madness, as in some fourth-category works, or the human interest might become so dominant as to eliminate the supernatural or lyrical elements, as in the contemporary plays. Finally, the demon plays produced an exciting and satisfying effect at the end of a program similar to that of the presto finale of a symphony. The Kyōgen farces staged between the plays did not break the mood so much as they gave the audience a temporary and welcome respite from the overpowering emotions of the tragedies.

Audiences today are not often prepared to spend the eight or more hours at the theatre that a complete program of Nō and Kyōgen would require. Often a program consists of three Nō and a single Kyōgen. The sedate god plays are performed relatively seldom, and even the woman plays, long termed the "rice bowl" of the actors, figure less frequently on the programs than plays of the fourth and fifth categories. But an over-emphasis given to the more exciting Nō plays tends always to weaken the effect and even defeat the purpose of the art. If the audience is not prepared spiritually by slower, more symbolic works before it sees a play like *Ataka*, the experience will hardly differ from seeing *Kanjinchō*, the Kabuki play derived from *Ataka*. It is not only forgivable but perhaps even necessary that the spectators be bored or made drowsy by a program of Nō. The plays are works of such lofty aspirations that a certain magnitude and even tedium is part of the total effect. If the audience has sat through a full program, its reaction to *Ataka* when presented as the fourth work will not be simple enjoyment of the exciting story and interesting characters; the audience will see *Ataka* as part of the world permeated by the atmosphere of Nō. Dramatic excitement is an element in Nō, and the stories have a concentrated intensity which rivals that of any stage, but Nō is prized above all for what it and no other theatre can achieve.

The special vocabulary of Nō makes discussion difficult for the uninitiated. The term *yūgen* is especially important as a criterion of Nō, but its meaning is not easy to define. Originally *yūgen* meant "dark" or "obscure" with overtones of mystery. It was frequently employed in Japanese poetic criticism of the twelfth century to describe beauty which is suggested rather than stated. There is *yūgen* in this famous poem by Fujiwara no Shunzei:

yū sareba	Evening has come;
nobe no akikaze	The autumn wind from the fields
mi ni shimite	Cuts into the flesh
uzura naku naru	And the quails are calling now
Fukakusa no sato	In Fukakusa Village.

The atmosphere evoked in this poem is lonely rather than inviting, monochromatic rather than colorful, but beneath the externals one may glimpse a deeply-felt beauty. Poets of this school felt that the emotions aroused by more conventionally admired sights were real but limited, but there was no limit to what might be evoked through suggestion. A monochrome suggests more than the most brilliantly tinted landscape; the evening in autumn evoked by Shunzei's poem is eternal and universal, not the happy or sad experience described by one man alone.

The ideal of *yūgen* shifted in meaning during the three centuries between Shunzei and Zeami. The word came to mean "charming" or "graceful" and was used, for example, to describe dancing boys at a shrine or even the traditional court football *(kemari)*. When Zeami himself attempted to define *yūgen* by giving examples from the manners, appearance and speech of people he knew, he chose the courtiers, and indicated that *yūgen*, at least at this period of his career, meant "grace" or "elegance." His insistence that Nō be filled with *yūgen* may have meant no more, then, than that it should aim at graceful expression even when representing ugly or frightening characters, unlike harsher and cruder types of theatre. The grace of an old woman or even a demon—let alone a beautiful woman—is certainly apparent in contemporary performances. In part this is due to the use of masks, but in Zeami's day the physical beauty of the actors, especially the boys who performed without masks, must have contributed much to the *yūgen*. Zeami himself, as a boy of eleven, attracted the attention of the young Shogun Yoshimitsu in 1374, and Yoshimitsu's infatuation (as much as his interest in the theatre) occasioned the patronage which the shogunate was to bestow on Nō for almost five hundred years. The plays provide for an unusually large number of children's roles, probably for this reason. Grace and beauty in the appearance of the actors, achieved if necessary by wearing masks, and in the language of the texts made up much of Zeami's *yūgen*.

But it is hard to imagine that Zeami meant nothing more profound by the term. In Zeami's later critical works *yūgen* takes on a darker coloration, and this return to the earlier poetic ideal has remained its prevailing meaning. If a critic says of a woman play that it possesses *yūgen*, he clearly does not mean merely that it is gracefully written or that the actor performed attractively. *Yūgen* in fact tends to reject conventional notions of beauty: if a display of feminine grace on the Nō stage were the highest aim, real women could now take the parts, though they were not permitted on the stage in Zeami's day. But the thought of a woman performing the role of, say, the courtesan Eguchi is repugnant to lovers of Nō who insist that a man in his sixties with a cracked bass voice and large, ugly hands has more *yūgen*. They are right: anyone who saw Kita Roppeita dance the role of the *shite* in *Sagi* ("The White Heron"), a man in his eighties taking the part of a bird, surely sensed the mysterious, indefinable presence of *yūgen*.

It is impossible to tell how Zeami's changing conceptions of *yūgen* may have been reflected in his works; though his criticism is dated, the plays are not. The texts of the plays in any case have been much altered. Zeami himself advocated that plays constantly be modified to suit the tastes of successive audiences. Zeami is now credited with authorship of only some twenty-five of the plays, though formerly he was believed to have written about half the plays in the repertory. Ironically, only one play of the third category, *Izutsu*, is now definitely attributed to Zeami, though the woman plays embody most perfectly his ideal of *yūgen*. Perhaps further research will restore to Zeami some of the masterpieces now labelled "of unknown authorship"; if not, we may become aware of the existence of one or more playwrights no less gifted than Zeami. Even in this unlikely case, Zeami's supreme importance in Nō will remain unshaken, not only because of the place he occupies in the historical development but because of his critical writings.

Zeami says disappointingly little about the composition of his plays even in his critical work devoted specifically to the subject, but his analysis of the art of acting is superb. Zeami's enumeration of the nine levels of actors reveals his philosophical as well as practical grasp of the art:

"*The Art of the Flower of Mystery*. This can be symbolized by the phrase, 'In Silla at midnight the sun is bright.' It is impossible to express in words or even to grasp in the mind the mystery of this art. When one speaks of the sun rising at midnight, the words themselves do not explain anything; thus too, in the art of Nō, the *yūgen* of a supreme actor defies our attempts to praise it. We are so deeply impressed that we do not know what to single out as being of special excellence, and if we attempt to assign it a rank, we discover that it is peerless artistry which transcends any degrees. This kind of artistic expression, which is invisible to ordinary eyes, may be what is termed the Art of the Flower of Mystery.

"*The Art of the Flower of Profundity*. This can be symbolized by the verse, 'Snow has covered the thousand mountains; why does one lonely peak remained unwhitened?' Someone long ago once said, 'Mount Fuji is so high that the snow never melts.' A Chinese, hearing this, criticized the expression as inadequate and insisted that one should say instead, 'Mount Fuji is so deep that the snow never melts.' Anything which is extremely high is also deep. One might also say, perhaps, that there is a limit to how tall a thing can be, but the depth, being limitless, cannot be measured. Perhaps that is why the immeasurable wonder of a landscape in which, though a thousand mountains are buried in snow, one peak alone remains unwhitened can be taken as an equivalent of the Art of the Flower of Profundity.

"*The Art of the Flower of Stillness.* This can be symbolized by the words, 'Snow piled in a silver bowl.' The whiteness and purity of snow piled in a silver bowl is truly a lovely sight: may we not say it represents the Art of the Flower of Stillness?

"*The Art of the Flower of Correctness.* This can be symbolized by the words, 'The mist is bright, and the sun sinks, turning the countless mountains crimson.' The vast panorama of countless mountains sharply defined in bright colors by the light of the sun shining on the world from a perfectly clear sky represents the Art of the Flower of Correctness. The artistic rank of this art is superior to that of Versatility and Precision, and is the rank of an actor who has already mastered a flower of the art of Nō and entered its domain.

"*The Art of Versatility and Precision.* This can be symbolized by the words, 'To tell completely of the clouds on the mountains, the moon on the sea.' The intent to depict completely the vast spectacle of nature is most surely present in the training for the Art of Versatility and Precision. This art is the turning point where the actor either advances to the higher ranks or falls back.

"*The Art of Faint Patterns.* This can be symbolized by the words, 'The Way that can be explained is not the eternal Way.' The actor should first learn to tread the eternal way and then learn of the Way that can be explained. By 'faint patterns' is meant that the actor, still not deeply etched with the art, shows its first beauty. This Art of Faint Patterns is considered the entry into the study of the Nine Levels.

"*The Art of Strength and Delicacy.* This can be symbolized by the words, 'The metal hammer moves, the precious sword glints coldly.' The movement of the metal hammer suggests the strong movements of this art. The coldness of the glint of the precious sword suggests an astringent style of acting, one suited to the discriminating spectator.

"*The Art of Strength and Crudity.* This can be symbolized by the words, 'The tiger, three days after it is born, is ready to devour an ox.' The strength displayed by the tiger in being disposed barely three days after its birth to eat an ox suggests the strength of this art. 'Eating an ox' indicates its roughness.

"*The Art of Crudity and Coarseness.* This can be symbolized by the words, 'The innate faculties of the flying squirrel.' Confucius said, 'The flying squirrel has five talents. It can climb a tree, swim in the water, dig a hole, fly and run. But these five talents are appropriate to the level of the flying squirrel; it performs none of them well.' When art lacks delicacy it can be said to be crude and a distortion of the true qualities."

Zeami's descriptions are elusive but there can be no doubt that he knew exactly what he meant. The highest "flower"—by "flower" Zeami seems to have designated the particular beauty an actor displayed—is that of "mystery." Though not a commonly mentioned aesthetic ideal in Western performing arts (technique, "sincerity," emotional intensity, etc. would be more common standards of excellence), it is not difficult to understand. Perhaps the closest embodiment of this ideal among twentieth-century artists was Greta Garbo, who managed always to remain inviolate, untouched by the vulgarity of the world around her, mysterious and supremely beautiful. The next highest flower is that of the master actor, a superbly accomplished performer, who deliberately admixes an element of imperfection into his art lest audiences become bored with too great, unrelieved perfection: the single unwhitened peak is this coarser element, lending greater allure to the many peaks covered by the flawless snow of *yūgen*. The art of Sarah Bernhardt, to judge from contemporary accounts, had qualities suggesting this "flower." The next flower, that of stillness, may bring to mind the voice of Elizabeth Schumann—absolute purity, lacking the touch of vulgarity that might have made her a supreme artist or destroyed her. "Snow piled within a silver bowl" is perfectly evocative of the stillness and mystery of *yūgen* incarnate.

As one descends further Zeami's nine levels, mystery and purity yield to accuracy and, finally, energy. Zeami insisted that an actor must begin his training not with the crude vigor of the bottom levels but about halfway up the scale, with the "Art of Faint Patterns." He studies the "two arts" (singing and dancing) and the "three roles" (the warrior, the woman and the old person) and improves his acting ability until he can be said to have attained the level of versatility and precision. If he achieves these qualities, he may be able to display the first of the "flowers," that of correctness, the level of the highly competent, professional actor. If he fails to display this flower, he will drop to the lower levels of performers, where he can still be a useful member of a troupe in roles requiring stamina or acrobatic skill. Had he started at the bottom levels, however, without having received the training suited to the higher roles, he would not be qualified to perform even roles of a more superficial nature.

Zeami considered *yūgen* to be the touchstone of his school of acting, but he did not ignore *monomane*, "imitation of things." The actor must perform the three roles convincingly to appear frightening as a demon or pathetic as a beggar. Despite the highly stylized nature of Nō performances, details needed to create a convincing character are not overlooked, as we can tell most easily from adverse comments. Here is how Shūō, the author of the seventeenth-century book of criticism *Bushō Goma*, denounced an actor who had played Shizuka in *Funa Benkei*: " 'I thought I would accompany you wherever you might go, but a feeble comfort, not to be depended on, is the human heart. Alas, there is nothing I can do!' are lines where the character weeps, but this hard-hearted Shizuka showed not the least inclination to weep. The woman does not exist who does not weep when she thinks she may never again see the man she was prepared to accompany to the ends of the earth."

Many similar examples could be found in the criticism written today. The actor playing Shizuka must be sufficiently versed in *monomane* to corroborate every phrase of the text, not with the literalness of the gesture-language of the dances of India, but within recognized, symbolic terms. He must not, on the other hand, forfeit the mysterious beauty of *yūgen* in the interests of convincing realism; an actor who attempted to persuade us he was really Shizuka by imitating a feminine voice, swaying seductively as he walked, or weeping convulsively, would be unspeakably vulgar on the Nō stage. Skill at *monomane* means a mastery of the symbols of the parts. The genius of a particular actor enables him to make these symbols seem exactly appropriate, so that when the blind Yoroboshi appears on the stage the angle of his head at a certain moment (certainly not any gesture of sniffing) exactly suggests that he has caught the scent of plum blossoms, telling him as he wanders in the dark of his blindness that he has reached his destination, the Tennōji Temple. An actor is usually able in the latter part of his career to embody in his performance the combination of *monomane* and the *yūgen* fitting each role; only then can he be called a master actor.

Zeami, like his father Kannami, was at once playwright, actor, and composer, a practical man of the theatre who took into account both his audience and the actors he worked with. His audience consisted chiefly of aristocrats who, he could assume, possessed an expert acquaintance with Nō and a sensitivity to slight variations in performance; they also were familiar with the original literary texts from which the plays derived and with earlier plays on the same subjects. Zeami wrote, "Many of the recent Nō plays have been based on old Nō, and are revised versions set to new music. . . . They stem from seeds which are capable of blossoming brilliantly at any time; it is necessary only to change the words somewhat and add a new flavor to the music so as to accord with the tastes of a different age. The Nō plays of the future should also be written in accordance with their times and prevailing tastes." The plays, then, had to meet the demands of the audience, but this did not mean playing down to their level; Zeami's experience in the theatre convinced him that actors with *yūgen* (rather than those with cruder, more striking talents) enjoyed the most lasting popularity. The author was no less bound by the actors; Zeami declared that "in composing Nō the most important thing is to write parts suited for the available actors." We know little about the actors of Zeami's troupe, but we can infer that *Atsumori* and *Kiyotsune* were written for young actors. An old actor in such parts, as Zeami pointed out, would not convince the audience even if disguised by a mask and youthful attire. But Zeami created his greatest works for older actors. He occasionally used the word *hie* ("chill") to describe the *yūgen* of the old actor. The term, also found in the literary criticism of Zeami's day, seems to have meant an interiorization of *yūgen*, an invisible *yūgen* which is no longer external grace or charm but comes from within. This highest development of *yūgen* has remained the actor's goal, and is still appreciated by audiences more than the most dazzling virtuoso display. Great actors possess this *yūgen*; it is instantly recognized by spectators, even those witnessing Nō for the first time; it never disappears.

Zeami thought that even demons should be represented with *yūgen*, and grudgingly admitted that actors of Kyōgen, which he seems to have held in low esteem, might be said to possess *yūgen* if their comedies amused audiences without descending into vulgarity. Zeami's disapproval of low comedy may account for the remarkably clean humor of Kyōgen, certainly when compared to the European medieval farces. In Zeami's day the plays may have been largely impromptu, with some admixture of obscene or slapstick comedy, but today the texts have considerable literary finish and the lines are delivered with a meticulous attention to clarity of diction which is unique among the Japanese theatrical arts. Kyōgen places little emphasis on singing and dancing, though both are present. The plays are essentially dependent on dialogue and the antithesis of the characters, rather than on the aura given off by a single character as in Nō. The roles are types, rather in the manner of the commedia dell'arte, but the range is severely limited by the conditions which prevailed in Japan at the time. Japan was virtually isolated from the rest of the world, and the occasional Chinese or Korean who made his way to Japan in the fifteenth or sixteenth century was much too uncommon a sight to figure in the farces. This meant that Kyōgen, unlike the European farces, made virtually no use of the comic possibilities of the foreigner—the amorous Frenchman, the reserved Englishman, the uncouth American, and so on. Isolation was not the only reason for the absence of foreigners: the humor of Kyōgen is essentially vertical, depending on the complications in the relations between master and servant rather than on the horizontal relations between two servants, two masters, or two people from different countries. In Kyōgen, moreover, rustics are funny not because of their accents (all persons of the same station tend to talk in exactly the same language) or the use of Japanese equivalents of zounds! or gadzooks! but because they behave inappropriately to their station. (The rustic baron cannot compose poetry decently.) The most frequent comic situation revolves around a foolish master and his clever servant. Invariably, the servant manages to trick the master, who realizes he has been duped only when it is too late. The successes of servants over masters have been cited by some scholars as expressions of protest by the lower classes. A few plays would seem to confirm this thesis, but common sense indicates that a farce would not be funny if it told of a clever master who gets the better of his hapless servant. The shoguns and their courts, the patrons of Nō and Kyōgen, would certainly never have tolerated satire of themselves if they thought it threatened their authority.

Kyōgen, like Nō, have been divided into categories, but they are less rigid. Only plays of the first category, the *waki* Kyōgen, are truly distinct; like the *waki* Nō they deal with gods or with auspicious occasions. The other categories include plays about daimyos, the great lords, and *shōmyō*, the lesser lords; about bridegrooms and sons-in-law; about devils or *yamabushi*, the fierce mountain ascetes; about priests and blind men, and so on.

Some Kyōgen, like *Uri-nusubito* ("The Melon Thief"), are constructed around a single farcical idea, others, like *Tsukimi Zatō* ("The Blind Man Looks at the Moon"), rise above the level of farce to that of a warm humanity. The best Kyōgen, as might be said of the best comedies anywhere, approach the borderline between comedy and tragedy, where we recognize the foibles of the characters but do not necessarily laugh at them. A few Kyōgen cross the borderline and are cruel rather than comic, but these are seldom performed.

The humor of Kyōgen stems mainly from the situations but, as we might expect in a theatre which places such emphasis on vertical relationships, it owes much also to the contrasting manner of delivery of characters belonging to different classes. Phrases which would have to be translated almost identically into English sound utterly different when pronounced by a daimyo or by Tarō-kaja, the servant, and some of the pleasure of Kyōgen comes from hearing the same lines pronounced in the strikingly dissimilar rhythmic patterns of master and servant.

The contribution of the actors to a performance is so overpowering that one tends to forget that Kyōgen must have had authors. Unlike Nō, we know virtually nothing about who wrote the Kyōgen plays, though many have been attributed to the learned priest Gen'e (1270–1350) or to Komparu Shirōjirō (d. 1473). These attributions, repeated to this day, are no longer seriously believed because so little evidence supports them. Perhaps these men supplied the germs of the plays with which they are credited, but the plots are simple, and have unquestionably been much altered by the actors over the years.

Kyōgen, though performed in close connection with the Nō plays, bear little resemblance in plot, unlike the European interlude farces which often specifically derided the action of the tragedies they followed. Some Kyōgen plays require masks, mainly when the actor performs as a god or a devil, but the actors normally appear without masks or makeup. Performing in Kyōgen seems to impart a remarkably warm and amiable quality to the faces of aged actors. This impression may owe much to the imagination of the beholder, but an aged Kyōgen actor performing one of the major roles may well bring to mind Zeami's remark that even the humblest role should be crowned with flowers. The level of Kyōgen is humble when compared to Nō, but within its chosen domain it has developed into an art at once engaging and heartwarming, the other side of the tragic world depicted in Nō and its necessary complement.

II. THE HISTORY OF NŌ AND KYŌGEN

THE EARLY PERIOD

The Yōgō Pine in Nara provided a passage for the descent of Nō from the world of the gods to the world of men, and the dancer at the annual festival still re-enacts the birth of Nō beneath the tree, moving at the will of a god as his creature, a medium possessed of the divine spirit. It would be meaningless to discuss the dancer's skill or his powers of interpretation; he is supposed merely to allow the god to guide his movements. In former days it was customary for an entire village to participate in its festivals. There were no spectators, and any man might perform as the central figure of the festival, the god. Eventually, however, one villager was deemed to excel as the interpreter of the god, his vehicle, and he was chosen from then on to give corporeal form to the unseen divinity. Other villagers believed he would please the god by the beauty of his actions. The first actor, then, may have only gradually become aware that he was a man playing the part of a god; the first spectator was the god. The dancer performed with the hope that the god, satisfied with the representation of his own actions, would grant long life and prosperity.

In time other spectators were attracted, and the performance of the dances or playlets at the festivals came to be the responsibility of the most talented men. Stages were built within the precincts of Shinto shrines facing the main object of worship, and the actors served as celebrants of a religious rite intended to benefit either a whole village or else a particular donor.

We have yet to uncover documentary evidence revealing when plays recognizable as Nō originated. Certainly by the twelfth century *Okina* was being staged. This play contains both Buddhist and Shinto elements, inseparably intertwined. The two religions, though entirely different in origins and sometimes absolutely contradictory in teachings, had early been woven by the Japanese into a single faith. Far from attempting to resolve the differences between the optimistic, this-worldly Shinto and the prevailingly pessimistic, other-worldly Buddhism, the Japanese took from each religion what suited them best, ignoring the contradictions. A desire for long life makes little sense in terms of the Buddhist tenet that this world is a place of trial and suffering preparatory to the true life after death, but the Japanese prayed for long life anyway, guided by the Shinto love of this world. The plays often describe the Shinto gods, but a strong Buddhist coloring runs through them in the language, the allusions to Buddhist texts, and the underlying acceptance of such Buddhist concepts as the impermanence of life. However, the ghosts who play so prominent a part in the Nō plays, returning from the world of the dead to speak to the living, those fearsome presences who must be exorcised so that the living may escape harm, originate in folk beliefs unsanctioned by either Shinto or Buddhism. An ill-defined, shamanistic religion, sharing much with similar beliefs on the mainland of Asia, provided a core around which formal Shinto and Buddhist tenets accumulated.

The union between the two religions was demonstrated by the close association of Buddhist temples and Shinto shrines. The Kōfukuji Temple, which exercised jurisdiction over the Kasuga Shrine (the site of the Yōgō Pine), was the scene of many early dramatic presentations. Priests of esoteric Buddhism known as *shushi* (or "spell makers") performed songs and dances by way of making their magical rites more intelligible to the onlookers. The *shushi* priests, dressed in splendid robes befitting their ecclesiastical functions, attracted spectators as well as worshipers, and their performances acquired dramatic elements. Probably they were the first to present *Okina*. This baffling conglomeration of songs and dances may originally have been a presentation in entertaining form of a Buddhist text, but the meaning is now buried under the accretions of the centuries.

The performances by the *shushi* priests were accompanied by lighter diversions—acrobatics and the like—in which professional actors known as *sarugaku* appeared. These actors belonged to entirely different, secular traditions, though they were likewise attached to the Kōfukuji and other temples for financial support. Their art can ultimately be traced back to *gigaku*, a kind of dancing imported from China in 612 A.D. This oldest recorded Japanese stage entertainment has almost completely disappeared, but more than 220 *gigaku* masks are preserved. Fragmentary records suggest that a *gigaku* performance began with a procession of actors masked as lions, birds, "strongmen," barbarians, and so on, in all a dozen or more parts. The procession was followed by dances accompanied by flutes and drums: in one an actor masked as a bird executed a dance in which he pretended to be pecking for worms; in another a contest was portrayed between the "strongman" and the barbarian for the favors of a beautiful girl, ending in triumph for the "strongman," who leads off the barbarian by a rope tied to his penis. One *gigaku* entertainment that has survived is the *shishimai* (or "lion dance"), a popular feature of many festivals.

The Japanese court, in a mood of enthusiasm for all things Chinese, initially welcomed *gigaku* and commanded that youths be trained in the art. The high point in *gigaku* history occurred in 752, on the occasion of the ceremonies marking the inauguration of the Great Image of Buddha at the Tōdaiji Temple, when sixty *gigaku* performers appeared. Half a century later only two men were still qualified as *gigaku* artists. The court in the meantime had discovered a more decorous entertainment in *bugaku*, stately court dances. Two varieties of *bugaku* were introduced in the seventh century: "left dances" *(samai)*, imported from China, included Indian music; "right dances" *(umai)* were of Korean and Central Asian origin. The names "left" and "right" denoted the direction from which the dancers made their entrances. The *bugaku* dances were in some sense representational, depicting a moment of a longer story, such as the triumphal return of a king from battle, but so highly stylized that the surviving dramatic element is negligible.

The *bugaku* dances, still performed at the Imperial Palace and at certain Shinto shrines, impart a distinctly alien atmosphere, largely because of the exotic masks and costumes. The original Chinese or Korean dances have nevertheless been altered by Japanese influences over the centuries. *Bugaku* in turn influenced Japanese dramatic and musical arts, including Nō. The division of each *bugaku* piece into three musical sections of increasingly rapid tempo—the *jo*, *ha*, *kyū* of Nō—was perhaps the greatest influence. *Bugaku* was at its full maturity when first introduced to Japan, and because it continued to retain its alien character it became in time a petrified ritual which could only be repeated, not developed. The changes that occurred in *bugaku* were doubtlessly unintentional and even unnoticed. By the end of the twelfth century *bugaku* had become a palace ceremonial.

The variety of entertainment called *sangaku* had been introduced to Japan from China together with *bugaku*. *Sangaku* included feats of magic, acrobatics, juggling, animal shows, etc. A picture of one stunt survives: a dancing girl wearing high clogs crosses a rope strung between poles balanced on the chins of two recumbent men, the girl juggling as she walks. *Sangaku* playlets were on such themes as "The head clerk of a temple slips on the ice and loses his trousers" and "The nun Myōkō begs for swaddling clothes," probably satirical pieces deriding the distraction or incontinence of the Buddhist clergy. Other playlets, like "The clever repartee of a Kyoto man" or "An easterner's first visit to the capital," seem to have been skits contrasting the sophisticated ways of city-dwellers with the artlessness of rustics. We know little more than these outlines, mentioned in a work written about 1160, but they prove that *sangaku* (or *sarugaku*, as it was known in a corruption of the word) included plays with plots and dialogue as well as dances and acrobatics.

From the grab bag of variety entertainments performed by the *sarugaku* players would eventually develop Nō and Kyōgen. The secular *sarugaku* actors, rather like the mimes of medieval Europe, began as clowns and acrobats but in the end presented works of an exalted, religious nature. Even the name *sarugaku*, though written with characters meaning "monkey music," lost its comic flavor when the performers, ever eager to add to their repertory, borrowed the plays of the *shushi* priests and presented them as entertainment rather than as religious instruction. *Sarugaku* also absorbed influences from two other early theatricals, *dengaku* and *ennen*, which shaped it artistically.

Dengaku (or "field music") was the name originally given to the songs and dances performed by country people, at times as part of the harvest celebrations. *Dengaku* of this nature can still be seen at festivals all over Japan. The court nobles in Kyoto, always on the lookout for new diversions from their usual activities, heard of these country dances and invited the performers to the capital. If *dengaku* in the thirteenth century was no more engrossing than its counterparts today, the nobles must have been stupendously bored before they could derive pleasure from such crude and inartistic caperings. Be that as it may, the original *dengaku* dancers—farmers and priests— soon gave way to professional actors who modified the performances to accord with the tastes of more sophisticated audiences. The simple costumes formerly worn in *dengaku* were replaced by elegant robes, and the songs were embellished with poetic language. By the fourteenth century, when the provincial lords also began to sponsor *dengaku*, the staging had become quite elaborate. The expenses incidental to performances were indeed so enormous that the downfall of Hōjō Takatoki (1303–33), the regent for the shogun, has been attributed to his mania for *dengaku*. By Kannami's day *dengaku* and *sarugaku* had become similar arts, much influence passing between the two. *Dengaku* failed to keep pace with *sarugaku*, perhaps because of the historical accident that it had no outstanding performers during the crucial period when Kannami and Zeami were developing *sarugaku* into a great dramatic art.

Ennen, the name of the other early dramatic form which influenced *sarugaku*, means "prolong years." It originated as ceremonies of prayer for the prolongation of some exalted person's life, but as early as 1100 the *ennen* prayers were followed by dances. The dances developed into plays by the fourteenth century. An account of *ennen* performances in 1429 indicates that the plays, in highly poetic language, were staged with ornate sets. *Ennen* influenced Nō by providing a model of how old songs, quotations from religious and secular literature, and a vocabulary including words of Chinese as well as Japanese origins might impart to the texts a dignity and beauty not found in older forms of drama. Probably each innovation in *sarugaku*, *dengaku* or *ennen* was quickly adopted by the others, making it difficult to distinguish among these arts. On the other hand, slight differences in the manner of recitation or dance were elevated into secrets by performers whose livelihoods might depend on their possessing (or seeming to possess) unique traditions. Already in Kannami's day there were four troupes of *sarugaku* actors in the province of Yamato: Yūsaki (founded by Kannami himself), Tohi, Emai, and Sakato, the ancestors of the present Kanze, Hōshō, Komparu, and Kongō schools respectively. Three other *sarugaku* troupes performed in the province of Ōmi, and there were troupes of *dengaku* and *ennen*. In contrast to the rigidly partisan divisions characteristic of the schools of Nō in later times, relations among the different *sarugaku* and *dengaku* players apparently were friendly, and a member of one troupe often studied the acting techniques of another. But even in the early days each troupe took care not to fall behind the others in techniques or in patrons.

Whatever the form of theatre, the most important factor in its development was the patronage of the upper classes. Without the backing of the nobles, *dengaku* would have remained no more than the prancing and artless singing of the country festival; *sarugaku* acquired its dignity only when enabled to abandon the crude realism demanded by the provincial audiences in favor of the poetic beauty appreciated by the court. Not only did the nobility patronize the drama and the actors, but by 1250 nobles themselves were performing in *sarugaku* for their own amusement. The future of *sarugaku* as the exalted art of Nō was determined in 1374 when Ashikaga Yoshimitsu, the shogun, attended performances at the Imakumano Shrine in Kyoto. On that occasion Kannami, then forty-one, appeared in *Okina* as the old man, and his son, later known as Zeami, in the role of Senzai. Yoshimitsu, entranced, lent his patronage to both father and son. Kannami, who had formerly toured the provinces with his troupe, was assured of court protection and was enabled to write plays not for illiterate farmers but for the most discriminating audiences.

YOSHIMITSU AND NŌ

Ashikaga Yoshimitsu was only seventeen when he witnessed the performances at Imakumano, but he was unquestionably the outstanding man in the entire country, not only by virtue of his office—Barbarian Quelling Great General—but because of his remarkable intelligence and ability. Yoshimitsu, the grandson of the founder of the Muromachi shogunate, did not forsake the martial traditions of his ancestors, as so often happened by the third generation, but he possessed also the literary and cultural talents of the courtier. He was an expert *tanka* poet (a number of his poems were selected for the imperially-sponsored anthologies), accomplished in linked verse *(renga)*, Chinese poetry, music, and Zen philosophy. He enjoyed travel, combining the business of consolidating his power over the country with his pleasure in excursions to Mount Fuji, the Inland Sea or the Great Shrine of Ise. As shogun he not only represented the apex of power during the Muromachi period (1336–1568) but ranks among the most powerful men of Japanese history. His success in military affairs was crowned by his reunification of the country in 1392 after sixty-four years of bitter division. Yoshimitsu has nevertheless been treated as a traitor by Japanese historians because his passion for things Chinese induced him to accept the title "King of Japan" bestowed on him by the Chinese court. His treatment of the imperial family, by no means reverent, has also aroused condemnation. Despite his failings, however, Yoshimitsu was a remarkable combination of martial statesman and aesthete.

Yoshimitsu's passion for Nō continued throughout his life. His patronage was extended not only to Zeami but to Dōami, a rival *sarugaku* actor, and to Kyōgen performers. His thorough grasp of poetic tradition and Buddhist language allowed Zeami to enrich his texts with a vocabulary and imagery of startling complexity. Yoshimitsu himself never performed, but he enjoyed theatrical display, as we know from the diary of his visit to Itsukushima, when he embarked wearing a "narrow-sleeved, wide-hemmed costume of a pale blue lozenge pattern tied with a red sash, green leggings and red knee-length breeches." This bizarre attire, the current craze among city dandies, excited comment, but was typical of Yoshimitsu's eccentric taste in dress.

Yoshimitsu abdicated the office of shogun in 1394 and took Buddhist orders the following year, but remained in control of the government. He also maintained his interest in *sarugaku*, an enthusiasm he transmitted to his son, the shogun Yoshinori, creating the tradition that the shogun, whatever his tastes, would protect Nō. Yoshimitsu may have found Nō brick, but he certainly left it marble.

KANNAMI AND ZEAMI

Yoshimitsu had probably already heard of Kannami when he decided for the first time in his life to attend a *sarugaku* performance and commanded that the most accomplished, rather than the senior, actor of the troupe should appear in *Okina*; he wished to see Kannami in the role. Kannami performed with such success that he was elevated to the position of "companion" *(dōhōshū)* to Yoshimitsu, sharing this distinction with other notable artists of the day. Kannami, however, never renounced his earlier audiences; he died in 1384 while on a tour of Suruga, an eastern province. Zeami spoke of his father with the utmost reverence, whether as an actor, composer, choreographer or playwright, but Kannami's greatest single contribution to the development of Nō may have been the incorporation into the plays of *kusemai*, a dance to an irregular, strongly-accented rhythm. *Kusemai* was to figure as the climactic, narrative section of most Nō plays, adding far more complexities of plot than the older dramatic forms permitted. Kannami is credited also with many celebrated works of the repertory, including *Matsukaze, Sotoba Komachi, Kayoi Komachi*, and *Eguchi*. Some critics claim that Kannami's style was simpler and directer than Zeami's, but little evidence supports this. *Jinen Koji*, it is true, startles at times by its realism, but *Matsukaze* and *Eguchi* reach summits of poetry rarely surpassed by later Nō dramatists. Kannami's plays were often adaptations of older works, and were in turn revised and augmented by Zeami and later men, leaving in the end only elements of Kannami's distinctive style; the eight or ten surviving plays believed to have been written by Kannami show few mutual resemblances, and stand apart also from later works. Scholars have argued that in the earliest Nō only one character, the *shite*, was of consequence, but *Kayoi Komachi* develops from the antithesis between the *shite*, Shii no Shōshō, and the *tsure*, Komachi; and *Sotoba Komachi* includes a theological dispute between the *shite*, Komachi, and the *waki*, a priest. The works attributed to Kannami suggest dramatic possibilities which most later dramatists rejected. Kannami's importance is unquestionable, but because he left no critical or autobiographical writings, most of what we know about him derives from his son's lavish but unverifiable praise.

Far more is known about Zeami. He emerges indeed as a distinct historical figure, though the basic biographical data is missing or incomplete. Our only source of information for his birthdate is the statement made in 1432 that he had reached his seventh *chitsu*, a word meaning decade; the words have therefore been interpreted as signifying that Zeami was then seventy years of age by Japanese reckoning, or sixty-nine by ours, fixing his date of birth at 1363. The six hundredth anniversary of his birth was accordingly celebrated in 1963, only for a new theory to be published which claimed that 1364 was correct. If this is correct, other dates must be shifted accordingly, placing the Imakumano performances in 1375 instead of 1374; but whichever the year, Zeami was eleven when he first appeared before Yoshimitsu.

Eleven is now considered too young for an actor to appear in adult roles, but Zeami believed that this was the time to begin mastering the repertory. "His childish appearance will give him *yūgen*, whatever role he may take. At this age too his voice is charming. These two advantages will make people forget his defects and call attention to the development of his qualities." By the time the actor is sixteen or so his voice has changed and he will have lost the "flower" of the boy performer. "Now that he is taller his charm has disappeared; it is no longer so easy for him to escape criticism because of the beauty of his voice and his physical charm." The emphasis Zeami gives to the beauty of the boy actor reflects the contemporary partiality, especially in samurai society, for young boys. Senzai, the role danced by Zeami before Yoshimitsu, is still assigned to the handsomest actor of a company, who dances without a mask. We know how much Zeami attracted Yoshimitsu from the account written by a nobleman in 1378, which describes Yoshimitsu taking Zeami to see the Gion Festival. Special stands had been erected for the Shogun and Zeami to watch the floats passing down Shijō, the main avenue. "The Shogun was accompanied by a boy, a Yamato *sarugaku* player, who watched the festival from the Shogun's box. The Shogun, who has for some time bestowed his affection on this boy, shared the same mat and passed him food from his plate. These *sarugaku* performers are no better than beggars, but because this boy waits on the Shogun and is esteemed by him, everyone favors him. Those who give the boy presents ingratiate themselves with the Shogun. The daimyos and others vie to offer him gifts, at enormous expense. A most distressing state of affairs."

At nineteen Zeami was already an established actor when he succeeded in 1384 as head of the troupe, following his father's death. Zeami seems, however, to have fallen into a slump afterwards; in *Kadensho* ("The Book of the Transmission of the Flower") he describes in terms that suggest autobiography the ridicule which the public often directs against an actor between the ages of seventeen and twenty-four, a period when his youthful charms have disappeared but his powers as a full-fledged actor have not yet emerged. During this critical period the actor must summon up all his resolve to keep from abandoning Nō altogether, in despair.

Zeami apparently recovered from his depression during his middle twenties, when he achieved recognition as an outstanding performer. He wrote, "By this period the actor's voice has settled completely, and his body has assumed its adult proportions. . . . People begin to notice him and to comment on his skill. He may be awarded a prize in a competition, even against actors of considerable ability, the public being delighted by the freshness of the talent he displays on that occasion. The public and the actor himself may then begin to think he is truly accomplished, but this is most detrimental to the actor. His is not a true 'flower'; he is merely in the prime of his youth, and the audience has been momentarily captivated by his charm. The true connoisseur will recognize the difference." The actor, in order to avoid serious harm to his career, must not let himself be deluded by flattery, but study all the harder the techniques of older actors, particularly *monomane*, "the imitation of things."

Zeami, in his middle thirties when he wrote *Kadensho*, described this as the culminating period of the actor's career. If he has still not won public recognition, he clearly has not acquired a genuine "flower," and his abilities will presently deteriorate. Zeami insisted on public recognition as the gauge of an actor's talents; the actor's function is to please the audience, and it alone will ultimately judge his merits. Zeami believed that the actor who had established a solid reputation by his middle thirties might preserve his "flower" even when his physical beauty began to fade in his forties. A truly remarkable performer, like Kannami, who appeared on the stage just a few weeks before his death in his fifty-second year, may still dazzle an audience though his repertory and range of color are now drastically limited by his age. (Zeami would probably have been astonished to see contemporary performances in which an actor in his sixties still takes the parts of beautiful young women.) Zeami likened the talent of the aged actor to flowers still blossoming on an aged tree with few remaining leaves.

In 1399, the year before writing *Kadensho*, Zeami appeared in festive performances of Nō attended for three days by the new shogun, Yoshimochi. The great success he scored on this occasion clearly established him as the leading *sarugaku* actor. It was a logical moment for him to take stock of his art. Most of Zeami's opinions concerning acting techniques were admittedly derived from his father; his purpose in writing *Kadensho* was, in fact, to preserve for his descendants the teachings of Kannami. The emphasis on *monomane* found throughout this work reflects Kannami's experience as an actor who habitually appeared before a public which demanded believable representation. Zeami in this work reveals himself as a practical man of the theatre whose desire to please his audiences took precedence over interpretative or aesthetic matters. He wrote, for example, that if persons of quality happen to arrive early for a performance it is improper not to begin immediately; if, on the other hand, exalted persons arrive towards the close of a performance their presence will so affect the audience that the usual order of plays must be altered.

Zeami contrasted the *sarugaku* styles of Yamato, which emphasized *monomane*, and of Ōmi, which gave priority to *yūgen*, considering elegance to be the basic element of Nō. This statement suggests how much Zeami's own art in his maturity was to be indebted to the Ōmi school; indeed, Zeami acknowledged that he owed much to Inuō (later known as Dōami), the leading Ōmi player. Inuō had first been introduced to Yoshimitsu by Kannami, and never forgot this kindness. His relations with Zeami were close, especially after Kannami's death, and the two men were almost equally respected as artists by Yoshimitsu. During the performances of Nō staged before the Emperor Go-Komatsu in 1408, on the occasion of his visit to Yoshimitsu's mansion at Kitayama, Zeami appeared on the eleventh of April and Inuō a week later. This was the apogee of Zeami's career as an actor. A month later Yoshimitsu fell ill, and on the thirty-first of May he died, in his fifty-first year. This event came as a severe blow to Zeami: Yoshimitsu had not only been a generous patron of Nō but its most discerning critic. Komparu Zenchiku, Zeami's son-in-law, wrote of Yoshimitsu that he had seen all the actors from Yamato and Ōmi, and could distinguish their qualities, "rejecting the crude and vulgar and insisting on *yūgen*." Yoshimitsu, we are told, "searched into the old and understood the new . . . He was scrupulously fair when it came to the arts." *Sarugaku* might have remained a folk entertainment but for Yoshimitsu's financial and artistic support, which enabled Zeami to develop it into a complex and elevated art.

Yoshimitsu's successor, Yoshimochi, bestowed his patronage chiefly on a *dengaku* actor named Zōami. We can gather from Zeami's description that Zōami was unusually accomplished; he wrote that he all but wept with emotion at Zōami's performance, which he likened to the "flower of stillness." Yoshimochi's appreciation of Zōami is easier to understand than his coldness towards Zeami. During the decade from 1413 to 1423 Zōami and *dengaku* reigned supreme in Kyoto. A dozen or more benefit performances of *dengaku* attest its popularity; not a single *sarugaku* benefit occurred during those years. Zeami, in his fifties, wrote some of his finest criticism, including *Shikadōsho* ("The Book of the Way of the Highest Flower," 1420) and *Nōsakusho* ("The Book of Nō Composition," 1423). In these works Zeami seems less interested in the elements of a successful performance—the "flower" of the actor, the intrinsic interest of a play, or the novelty of presentation—than in the unchanging aesthetic values of Nō. He emphasizes the importance of the combination of song, dance and *yūgen*, the latter term having now shifted in meaning from "charm" to "mysterious beauty." Undoubtedly Zeami also composed Nō plays while writing these essays, but we cannot tell which works fall in this period.

In 1422 Zeami, having reached the age of sixty by Japanese reckoning, became a Buddhist priest and withdrew as head of his company, leaving the position to his son Motomasa, about thirty years old at the time. Zeami had one other son, Motoyoshi, for whom he wrote *Nōsakusho* and who in turn recorded Zeami's sayings in *Sarugaku Dangi* ("Conversations on *Sarugaku*," 1430). We can assume that he entertained high hopes for both sons. Motomasa quickly established himself as a superlative actor in Zeami's tradition, and his future seemed assured when a threat unexpectedly arose in the person of Zeami's nephew Motoshige. The latter's spectacular rise to fame began in 1427 when he was selected by Gien, the abbot-prince of the Shōren Temple, to appear in a benefit performance of Nō. On the death of Yoshimochi without heir in 1428, this same Gien, Yoshimochi's brother, returned to the laity to assume the office of shogun under the name Yoshinori. He too was hostile to Zeami and Motomasa and, as Motoshige's protector, was determined to make him first among the *sarugaku* actors. In August, 1428, at Yoshinori's command, Motoshige performed Nō at the Muromachi Palace. Neither Zeami nor Motomasa was invited. In 1429 Motomasa and Motoshige both appeared in plays staged on the riding grounds of the Muromachi Palace, spectacles distinguished by the use of "real horses and real armor," a far cry from the symbolic use of props that distinguishes Nō today. Ten days later Yoshinori issued an order forbidding Zeami and Motomasa from appearing at the palace of the Retired Emperor; from then on Motoshige gave the New Year's performances for the Retired Emperor. In 1430, again by order of Yoshinori, Motomasa was dismissed from his post as Master of Music at the Kiyotaki Shrine and replaced by Motoshige. Motomasa, dismayed by these repeated indications of Yoshinori's hostility, left Kyoto to live in the hinterland of Yamato Province. Towards the end of the same year, 1430, Zeami's second son, Motoyoshi, gave up the stage to become a priest.

These events were terrible blows to Zeami, but the worst was yet to come: in 1432 Motomasa suddenly died. A month later Zeami wrote a final tribute:

"'To the roots the blossoms return, to old nests the birds hurry back; will the spring go the same way too?' This expression of love for the blossoms and envy for the birds must surely have been written by a man of feeling. I have known such inconsolable grief for the beloved son I have lost that I have envied the mindless blossoms and birds; the color of the blossoms and the songs of the birds have brought me only pain and uncertainty. I realize now, however, that the emotion involved must be the same.

"On the first day of the eighth moon my son Zenshun died at Anonotsu in Ise Province. It may seem foolish of me not to have resigned myself long ago to the fact that the young do not necessarily die after the old, but the blow came so unexpectedly that it quite overwhelmed my aged mind and body, and tears of grief rotted away my sleeves. Zenshun, though I say it of my own son, was an incomparable master of acting. Long ago my late father established our family name in this art, and I too, succeeding him, labored selflessly for it. Now I have reached my seventh decade. It seemed to me that Zenshun's talents surpassed even those of his grandfather, and I recorded for him all the secret traditions and mysteries of the art, remembering the text which says you must tell a man the truth while you can, for otherwise you may waste his talents. But all that I wrote down is now the dream of Rosen, and I have no choice but to let these teachings, which nobody will master and which will benefit no one, turn to dust and smoke. If I preserve them for posterity now, whom will they help? The sentiments described in the poem, 'Now that you are not here, to whom shall I show these plum blossoms?' are true indeed. But my grief is unendurable when I think that the destruction of our art is at hand, and that I must witness such a disaster with my own eyes, in the meaninglessness of the lingering last years of my life. Alas! Confucius was heartbroken at the death of his son, and when Po Chü-i was preceded in death by his son, they say he vented his hatred on the medicine still left by the boy's pillow.

"Zenshun came into this phantom world. For a moment we became father and son. Now, in grief over parting, I have scattered words aimlessly as leaves tumbling from a bough, truly a sign my grief is too much to bear. 'Did I ever dream it? That while I, a withered tree, linger in this world, I should see the fall of a flower in full bloom?'

9th moon, 4th year of Eikyō [1432]   Shiō [Zeami]

" 'If I did not think my life had a term, how could I know any end to the tears shed by this aged body?' "

Zeami's despair was eventually mitigated by the achievements of his son-in-law Komparu Zenchiku (1405–1468), his artistic successor and the heir to his teachings, but his despondency over Motomasa's death darkened this whole period of his life. Motomasa was not only a superb actor, as we know from Zeami's testimony, but a gifted dramatist. His surviving works include *Sumidagawa* and *Yoroboshi*, among the most affecting plays of the repertory; the unhappy circumstances at the end of his life may account for their strong element of pathos. After his death the headship of the Kanze school went to Motoshige (now known as Onnami), probably at Yoshinori's insistence. An account of the benefit performances staged in Kyoto in May, 1433, before Yoshinori and members of the imperial court suggests the lavish scale on which Yoshinori supported Onnami's art.

One further disaster awaited Zeami: in 1434 he was banished to the island of Sado. Yoshinori's reasons for exiling Zeami are not known, but his hatred must have been implacable indeed to send a man in his seventies to a distant, lonely island. Zeami probably remained on Sado until 1441 when a general amnesty was declared after the assassination of Yoshinori. Zeami's exile was lightened by the solicitude displayed by Zenchiku. After his return to Kyoto, Zeami apparently lived with Zenchiku until his death in 1444, at the age of eighty. While on Sado, Zeami wrote *Kintōsho*, a series of prose-poems describing his exile. One account reports that seven plays written by Zeami at the time were responsible for his securing pardon. The story is dubious, but it indicates at least that some plays may date from the last years of Zeami's life.

NŌ AFTER ZEAMI

The brutal assassination of Yoshinori while he was watching a performance of *sarugaku* is indicative of the unrest which seriously threatened the government. Yoshimitsu's authority had been absolute, but the strength of the shogunate was constantly eroded during the fifteenth century. Frequent uprisings against authority occurred throughout the country, the climax occurring with the Ōnin Rebellion of 1467 to 1477, when most of Kyoto was destroyed. After the rebellion the rule of the shogunate was largely a fiction.

The Nō theatre was a fitting form of drama for these chaotic times. The presence of ghosts and the world of the dead (as if they had displaced the living not only in importance but in reality) reflects the Buddhist conviction that this world is a place of foulness and corruption, a temporary dwelling before we move on to the more lasting realities of the life after death; it also suggests the agonizing uncertainty of a world where destruction was the rule and the heritage of the past had been reduced to ashes. In the first year of the Ōnin Rebellion, Ichijō Kanera, the Prime Minister and a great noble, was forced to go begging for food after his house and library, the repository of centuries, were wantonly destroyed. In such times it is not surprising that men turn to comfort promised beyond the grave.

Buddhist thought, though important in the works of Kannami and Zeami, becomes dominant both in the plays and essays of Komparu Zenchiku. Few details are known about Zenchiku's life, partly because he performed mainly in Nara, rather than in the capital, but records bear witness to his friendship with the leading Buddhist priests of the day, including the celebrated Ikkyū (1394–1481). One essay by Zenchiku is purely theological, a criticism of a certain Buddhist sect, and the others make frequent use of Buddhist terminology, explaining in metaphysical terms the nature of Nō. The search for a meaning beyond appearances, rejected as illusory, is found also in the works of Shōtetsu (1381–1459), a Buddhist priest and the best poet of his day. For him *yūgen* was that ultimate reality: "What we call *yūgen* lies within the mind and cannot be expressed in words. Its quality may be suggested by the sight of a gauzy cloud veiling the moon or by the autumnal mists swathing the scarlet leaves on a mountainside. If one is asked where *yūgen* can be found in these sights, one cannot say; a man who cannot understand this truth is quite likely to prefer the sight of the moon shining brightly in a cloudless sky. It is quite impossible to explain wherein lies the interest or wonder of *yūgen*." Clouds and mists, veiling the bare truths of a landscape, lend ambiguity and mystery, and suggest more than a brightly illuminated scene. The poet himself may not be able to explain the ultimate meaning of his words, but the sensitive person will detect and respond to something lying beneath the surface; what each man finds is likely to be different. If the sceptic dismisses the mystery as nothing more than the emperor's new clothes, or prefers crimson leaves radiant in the sunshine to glimpses of them through mist, one obviously cannot convince him that he is wrong.

The need that Zenchiku and Shōtetsu experienced to believe in the existence of some ultimate meaning behind the terrible spectacle of the world induced them to seek beauty which might be sensed if not described. Their preference for suggestion and mystery was shared by the masters of the tea ceremony, and by the landscape architects who created gardens bare of flowers or trees. Zen philosophy gave direction to their aestheticism. Zeami's critical writings showed an increasingly marked Zen coloration; with Zenchiku it became dominant. The aesthetics of Nō may owe more to Zenchiku than to Zeami: the bare stage, the insignificant props, the movements of the actors, recalling at once the Zen priest and the warrior. The overpoweringly sombre tone of the plays certainly brings to mind not Zeami's "flowers" but the gloom of a monochrome, flowerless world.

Zenchiku's successors, however, turned to realistic or dramatic themes with few symbolic overtones. The plays of Miyamasu treat mainly martial subjects; the characteristic works of Nobumitsu (1435–1516), like *Dōjōji* or *Momijigari*, are "demon" plays filled with violence; those of Kanze

Nagatoshi (1488–1541) often have such large casts as to make them resemble Kabuki more than Nō. Zenchiku's grandson, Komparu Zempō (c. 1474–c. 1520) wrote one play, *Hatsuyuki*, in the *yūgen* manner, but his characteristic vein was straightforwardly dramatic. Even at the court of the shogun in Kyoto the dramatists, unable to hope for a patron like Yoshimitsu, were obliged to entertain with works which pleased by their novelty and dramatic excitement. With the collapse of the shogun's power in the sixteenth century, the Nō troupes had no choice but to rely on popular support, and the general public was ever more insistent on dramatic action.

Even in the sixteenth century, however, Nō did not reject altogether its unique qualities in favor of theatrical excitement. It remained prevailingly a repertory theatre, and the different troupes continued to stage the works of Zeami and Zenchiku. Surviving records indicate that the individual plays most often performed were *Yuya*, *Kureha*, *Takasago*, and other relatively static works, though plays of the fourth and fifth categories as a whole were by far the most frequently staged. Evidently the public still appreciated the solemn beauty of some plays, though the bulk of the programs was given over to dramatic pieces.

Kojirō Nobumitsu's background as a *waki* actor probably accounted for the prominence of *waki* roles in his plays; in *Chōryō* and *Rashōmon* the *waki*'s part is more important than the *shite*'s, and in *Shōzon* by Nobumitsu's son Nagatoshi, the last important Nō dramatist, the distinction between *shite* and *waki* has become so arbitrary that the nomenclature varies today according to the school.

During the sixteenth century the schools of Nō emerged as distinct and sometimes hostile groups, each jealously guarding its particular traditions. The Kanze school had virtually monopolized performances given in the shogun's presence, but after the death of the Shogun Yoshihisa in 1489 and of the former Shogun Yoshimasa in 1490, the Ashikaga family lost control of the court. A relaxation of the rules of precedence enabled the other three schools of Nō—Hōshō, Komparu and Kongō—to participate in court performances. In 1493, for example, the Kanze and Komparu schools staged rival presentations at the shogun's palace, and in 1497 the Komparu and Kongō schools were pitted against each other. The Kongō and Hōshō schools hardly figure in the earlier history of Nō, but with greater opportunities to perform they now began to gain prominence.

Kongō Ujimasa (1507–1576), a colorful as well as talented performer, was known by the nickname of "Nose Kongō," apparently because of his large nose and nasal voice. The nickname occasioned the legend that he was once so determined to dance with the head of a certain Buddhist statue for his mask that he broke the head from the statue and made its face into a mask. He performed wearing this mask, only for a terrible boil soon to form on his nose; eventually the tip rotted away, giving Ujimasa his sobriquet. Legends aside, Ujimasa was a tempestuous figure, profiting by the new freedom in the world of Nō to assert himself and his school. In 1541 he had a bitter quarrel with the head of the Komparu school over precedence at the Kasuga Festival. He had his way, but two years later an even more violent dispute broke out, which aligned the Komparu, Kanze and Hōshō schools against the Kongō, forcing Kongō Ujimasa to yield. The Komparu and Kongō schools, though enemies on this occasion, generally resembled each other in their conservative style of performance. They were called *shimogakari*, which meant the style of Nara, in contrast to the *kamigakari*, or style of Kyoto, favored in Kyoto and practiced by the Kanze and Hōshō schools.

During the sixteenth century, Nō attained its greatest popularity with the general public, especially as performed by amateur actors. The imperial court, though poverty-stricken, was also devoted to Nō, but its tastes no longer swayed the actors. The scanty remaining evidence concerning Kyōgen in this period indicates that the farces had become established as an integral part of Nō programs, and that the texts, though still unrecorded, were gradually acquiring a fixed form, though improvisation had hitherto been the rule. Performances of Nō and Kyōgen by women were popular; they seem to have been received with equal enthusiasm in tragedy and comedy, suggesting that the audiences made little differentiation between Nō and Kyōgen, treating both with an irreverence which would have dismayed Zeami. New plays continued to be written, in response to a demand for novelty, but they failed to remain in the repertory. Despite its flourishing condition Nō had ceased to be a living dramatic form.

HIDEYOSHI AND NŌ

At the end of the sixteenth century Nō found a new patron in Toyotomi Hideyoshi (1536–1598), the self-made ruler of all Japan. After over a century of civil warfare, Hideyoshi succeeded in re-uniting the country and establishing an effective government. Once secure in his position, he felt he must prove that he was not culturally inferior to the nobles and priests; the best way, he decided, was to study Nō. He chose the Komparu school, probably under the influence of Shima-tsuma Shōshin (1551–1616), a priest and amateur actor who left some invaluable studies of Nō. Hideyoshi became passionately fond of the art, and other daimyos were obliged to study Nō in order to stay in Hideyoshi's good graces. In 1593, while Hideyoshi was in Kyushu waiting for the start of the invasion of Korea, he spent his time learning Nō, memorizing fifteen roles in the course of fifty days; before long he was confidently performing them before the public. On receiving word of the birth of his son, Hideyoshi hastily returned to Kyoto, and as part of the festivities himself performed for three days before the Emperor Go-Yōzei. Hideyoshi appeared in sixteen plays, including *Okina*, *Matsukaze*, and *Eguchi*. Tokugawa Ieyasu performed *Nonomiya*, and on the second day joined with Hideyoshi in a newly composed farce, *Kubihiki*.

Hideyoshi's passion for Nō reached its climax in 1594 when he performed at the imperial palace, not only in various classical works including *Sekidera Komachi*, the most difficult play of the entire repertory, but also in five new dramas written at Hideyoshi's order by his biographer Ōmura Yūko (d. 1596) to celebrate Hideyoshi's accomplishments. *Yoshino-mōde*, a "god" play, describes Hideyoshi's visit to the cherry blossoms of Yoshino. The *waki*, a courtier, explains at the beginning that Hideyoshi has ruled the country as he sees fit for three years and conquered Korea. Lately, moreover, he has won martial glory against the Chinese, desisting from warfare only at their earnest request. He has returned to the capital and built a great castle at Fushimi, and now has come to Yoshino to admire the cherry blossoms. In the second scene of the play the god of Yoshino appears and announces he will protect Hideyoshi on his return to the capital. *Shibata*, a warrior play, relates Hideyoshi's exploits in defeating Shibata Katsuie; the *shite*, the ghost of Shibata, describes how he triumphantly led his forces into Ōmi Province and seemed about to win a great battle when "Hideyoshi himself came riding up against us, and the tens of thousands on my side, slashed down by his sword, fled the field, unable to withstand him." The *shite* of *Kōya-mōde*, a "woman" play, is none other than Hideyoshi's mother. She appears first as a nun, but in the second scene reveals herself as a bodhisattva of song and dance, and informs us that she owes her salvation to the prayers of her filial son. Hideyoshi himself is the *shite* of *Akechi-uchi*, and the play concludes with a paean of praise for his martial prowess. *Hōjō* has virtually an identical plot. *Toyokuni-mōde*, written by another dramatist after Hideyoshi's death, is a fitting conclusion to the series of plays, presenting him as the god Toyokuni Daimyōjin. The *tsure* is Yūgeki, a Chinese general, who comes with tribute offerings for the god, declaring that Toyokuni Daimyōjin is worshiped not only in Japan but in China too.

The Nō plays written for Hideyoshi are typical of the man, but they suggest also the exuberance of the Momoyama period—the end of the sixteenth century—when Japan, after long years of warfare, enjoyed a rebirth of secular learning and pleasures. The military men threw themselves eagerly into cultural pursuits. The study of *The Tale of Genji* in particular developed into a craze, and Nō based on this novel (like *Aoi no Ue*) enjoyed the greatest popularity. The plays about Hideyoshi reflect his enormous pride in his cultural attainments. It would have been extraordinary in any theatre for an actor to perform as himself in a heroic drama, but the Nō theatre especially avoided any taint of contemporary realism; the dramas of Zeami and his successors were set in the past, either a remote, dateless antiquity or else the period of the twelfth-century wars. Hideyoshi's Nō plays describe events that had just occurred, pointing the way to the highly topical Kabuki and Bunraku plays of the seventeenth century.

We know of other startling changes in Nō from the letters of European missionaries in Japan at the time, who mention dramas on Biblical themes, apparently cast in the form of Nō. The addition of contemporary and foreign subjects and the use of dramatic forms which ignored the traditional division of parts into *shite* and *waki* and tended to make the chorus superfluous made it seem that Nō was about to break with the past and develop into a form of drama closer to that of Europe. In fact, however, precisely the opposite occurred.

TOKUGAWA NŌ

At the close of the sixteenth century the great cultural ferment created a demand for more theatrical entertainment. Two new forms of theatre, Kabuki and Bunraku, better suited to the general public than Nō, came into being and usurped the audiences from the older drama. There were hardly any benefit performances of Nō under Hideyoshi, a sure sign that it was fast becoming an upper-class entertainment, normally not open to the general public. After the death of Hideyoshi in 1598 the Nō actors were forced to look for new patrons. They turned not to the public but to Tokugawa Ieyasu. As soon as Ieyasu's castle in Edo (the modern Tokyo) was completed in 1606, the Kanze and Komparu troupes hurried to the scene, eager to perform for the Shogun. The Kongō and Hōshō schools followed the example, and in 1608 all four schools gave performances in the castle.

From this time on, Nō served as the official music of the Tokugawa regime. The shoguns, devoted to Confucian doctrines, considered rites and music to be essential elements of government, and just as *bugaku* had provided the ceremonial music for the emperor's court, the gravity and stately movements of Nō won favor at the shogun's court, which was run according to the decorum imposed by the Confucian code. The performances of Nō, especially at the New Year, were elaborate rituals believed to be capable of affecting the prosperity and welfare of the state. Skillful actors, because they contributed to the stability of the régime, were therefore provided with stipends in rice or money by the government and ranked as samurai. They lived far more luxuriously than most samurai because their incomes were frequently swelled by presents from the daimyos and other pupils. The gifts received after the first performances of the year might be so generous as to provide the leading actors with their living expenses for the entire year. However, the rulers were not only munificent patrons but exacting critics. They tolerated no idleness, let alone mistakes. An actor who committed a lapse during a festive performance was immediately and unsparingly punished; in extreme cases, actors were condemned to commit ritual disembowelment or were sent into exile for faulty performances. The severity of the punishments was not only inspired by aesthetic standards but by the belief that mistakes in the execution of the ritual music might lead to national calamity.

The outstanding actor of the early seventeenth century, Kita Shichidayū (1586–1653), had served Hideyoshi and fought against the Tokugawa at the battle of Osaka. So renowned was he as an actor, however, that his offense against the Tokugawa family was pardoned by the Shogun Hidetada. He was even granted permission to found a school of Nō bearing his name, the first new school since the time of Kannami. The Kita school, though derived from the Kongō, is still distinguished by its martial quality in performance. Shichidayū was by far the most popular actor at the shogun's court: in the year 1629 alone Hidetada requested him to appear in eleven special performances as against only one by another actor. In 1631, when Hidetada was stricken with a mortal illness, all five schools performed Nō by way of prayer for his recovery. The death of Hidetada deprived the Kita school of its protector, and the jealousy of the other schools threatened its existence. In 1634 Shichidayū's performance of *Sekidera Komachi* was denounced as being unorthodox and at variance with tradition, grave charges in a Confucian society. The Shogun Iemitsu, acting on the advice of the heads of the other schools, condemned Shichidayū to six months' imprisonment. He was released after special intercession in his behalf by the powerful daimyo Date Masamune, but seldom performed afterwards.

The shogun's government frequently showed its concern about Nō by directing admonitions to the actors. In 1647, for example, these commands were issued:

"Actors must not neglect the performing techniques handed down in the various schools. They should not indulge in inappropriate arts but devote themselves exclusively to preserving the traditions of their profession. They should in all things obey the directions of the head of the school; in the event of a lawsuit, they should request the head of the school to petition the authorities. Any misdemeanor on the part of the head should be reported at once to the authorities.

"On the occasion of command performances of *sarugaku*, the actors will be informed on the previous day. They should assemble at the residence of the head of the school, rehearse the works to be performed thoroughly, and make sure that there will be no mistakes on the following day.

"As repeatedly directed, actors should refrain from any display of luxury and should practice strict economy at all times. Their houses, clothing, food, etc. must be in keeping with their station and modest. Actors are forbidden to abandon their family careers and to learn the military or other arts unsuited to their station. . . .

"Actors should not accumulate unnecessary possessions beyond the costumes and equipment used in *sarugaku*.

"When invited to appear before nobles and other persons of quality they should not eat with their hosts.

"The Komparu school for generations has enjoyed renown. However, the present head of the school, though adult in years, in still immature as an artist. He should henceforth devote himself energetically to his art. Older actors of his school should help and guide him. Any further negligence on his part will be considered a misdemeanor."

It is hard to imagine any other government issuing an official edict of this nature, but the Tokugawa régime considered that it was just as important to its stability that actors perform the official music properly as for priests to offer prayers in an orthodox, acceptable manner. The necessary atmosphere of decorum and dignity implied a suitable magnificence of accoutrements, and the government, though insistent that actors refrain from luxury in their private lives, never prohibited extravagance in the Nō costumes, which became miracles of weaving and dyeing.

Initially, at least, the shogun's government welcomed the enthusiasm exhibited by the daimyos for Nō, preferring this peaceful avocation to warlike pursuits that might endanger the state. When the daimyos themselves began to perform Nō, however, the government felt obliged to issue admonitions, though appearing in Nō was obviously not as serious an offense as playing the samisen or singing popular songs. The daimyos continued to learn Nō without major interference. At the time of the revival of Nō in the late nineteenth century, several nobles ranking as daimyo appeared prominently in performances. Throughout the Tokugawa period, samurai of lesser rank were also active in Nō. Some performed at the Imperial Palace in Kyoto, where professional *sarugaku* actors were still treated as outcastes.

Nō was open to the general public from time to time in the form of benefit performances (*kanjin* Nō). In the Muromachi period such performances had genuinely been for the benefit of a temple or shrine, but in the Tokugawa period they came to be purely commercial ventures on the part of the actors. Most benefits required only the permission of the local magistrate, but there were also special "once-in-a-lifetime" benefits for outstanding actors, performances staged for the townsmen, who may have felt that attending Nō placed them higher up the social ladder than going to see Kabuki or Bunraku. In most respects these benefits were performed with the same degree of ceremonial as if before the shogun, but the press of the crowd was sometimes so intense that the stiff, formal holiday attire of the spectators was in danger of being ripped to shreds. Elderly people sent substitutes to hold their places, and these men, dressed in nondescript clothes, would cheerfully shout greetings to the shogun and other high officials when they arrived— "There's the chief!" "Best in Japan!" Such informality normally would have been unthinkable in the rigid society of Tokugawa Japan, but the theatre, like the gay quarters, was immune from the usual hierarchical demands, and the guards stationed inside the theatre made no attempt to suppress the rowdy spectators.

Because of the ritual nature of Nō during this period the repertory remained virtually static. Many plays were written, perhaps two thousand, but generally for a particular occasion and never repeated. None of the two hundred or more surviving plays of the period has been deemed worthy of a revival. The Tokugawa Nō plays, bound both in language and plots to the traditions of a departed age, are usually no more than pastiches of the mannerisms of Nō without any emotional involvement. The subjects were remote, the dramatists (unlike those of Hideyoshi's time) too timid to treat contemporary subjects. The best may actually be not inferior to some works in the current repertory, but the latter have at least the advantage of being genuine.

The elevation of Nō to the status of court ceremonial meant also that its dramatic appeal need no longer be considered. The dialogue, originally close to the tempo of speech, came to be pronounced in a deliberate, protracted manner, and the sung parts were delivered in muffled, almost unintelligible tones. The dances too were greatly prolonged, and moments when nothing occurred on the stage, save for an occasional beat of the drum and a strangled cry from the drummer, came to occupy as much as a quarter of the length of the play. The *monomane* elements were largely sacrificed. But, it may be argued, the slow, ritualistic presentation may have accorded better with Zeami's ideals than the livelier performances of his own day.

The extreme solemnity of Nō probably whetted the appetite of the spectators for Kyōgen as comic relief. During the Muromachi period Kyōgen was so unimportant that it was scarcely noticed by the diary writers who supplied detailed accounts of Nō; they treated the Kyōgen plays with the silent disdain of the learned film critic of today discussing a program of avant-garde masterpieces which happens to include a Donald Duck cartoon. During the Tokugawa period the Kyōgen actors ranked lowest among the performers associated with Nō, below the flutists and drummers, but thanks to the general patronage of the art as a ceremonial, Kyōgen acquired a measure of dignity. The texts were established for the first time and, inevitably it would seem, three distinct schools—Ōkura, Izumi and Sagi—insisted on their own versions. The new dignity did not destroy the humor of Kyōgen. On the contrary, a comparison of the oldest surviving texts with the definitive versions compiled later in the seventeenth century reveals that the comic features were sharpened and the satirical elements—the fun poked at pompous but foolish daimyos and the like—made more effective.

It may seem strange that the daimyos should not only have tolerated but enjoyed comedies in which they were the butt of the humor. Probably even in the Muromachi period they felt no class solidarity with the parvenu daimyos depicted so irreverently, finding them as absurd as the court of Louis XIV found the *petit marquis* of a Molière farce. In the Tokugawa period the members of the shogun's court could view with amusement and utter detachment the daimyo in *Kombu-uri* who, after forcing his servant to carry his sword, is compelled by the servant to sing like a peddler hawking his wares. It was inconceivable that any daimyo of the seventeenth century would be on terms of such familiarity with a servant.

The transcribing of the Kyōgen texts in the seventeenth century inhibited the improvisation which had always been part of its humor. It also petrified the humor: though far easier to understand than Nō, the language of Kyōgen had become archaic by the Tokugawa period and no longer could express effectively the amusing experiences of daily life. Most of the two hundred or so surviving Kyōgen plays depict Muromachi life, though revised versions of old works and, more rarely, new plays continued to be staged in the traditional manner.

The Kyōgen actors shared some of the glory surrounding Nō during the Tokugawa period. They had patrons among the daimyos and pupils even in the imperial court, but the comic relief they lent to a program must have been tolerated grudgingly by the sterner Confucianists of the court. The actors took their art extremely seriously, and if given less than due credit when they performed in the forbidding atmosphere of the shogun's presence, they came into their own before the crowds at a benefit performance.

The last and most spectacular of the gala benefits occurred in 1848, the "once-in-a-lifetime" performances given by the head of the Hōshō school. The shoguns, from the days of Yoshimitsu, had favored the Kanze school, but with the eleventh shogun, Ienari (1773–1841), the Hōshō school gained preference, and subsequent shoguns continued this patronage. Permission was granted to Hōshō Yagorō to stage benefit performances on fifteen clear days. The series began on March 6, 1848 but did not reach the fifteenth day until June 13, the rainy spring having interfered with the outdoor performances. An elaborate theatre seating five thousand spectators was constructed in Edo. The audiences consisted of an extraordinarily varied cross-section of Japanese society. The gentry and their wives paid three pieces of silver for the privilege of sitting in upstairs boxes protected from the public gaze by curtains of purple silk dyed with their family crests. The commoners paid two pieces of silver to sit below; but even upstairs, in locations with poor views of the stage, townsmen sat crosslegged in breeches and striped cloaks alongside country bumpkins in cotton kimonos and old women wearing aprons. The audience was at liberty to drink saké, but keeping one's head covered or stripping to one's underwear was strictly prohibited. The crowd downstairs included low-ranking samurai, lady shampooers, Confucian scholars, doctors, fortune-tellers, Shinto priests, poets and many others, all jammed together indiscriminately. Upstairs, the daimyos and their consorts observed the plays "set out in a row, like a display of penny dolls."

The audience was by no means respectful. When Hōshō Yagorō made his entrance, instead of the solemn silence we expect today there were cries of, "Here's the man from Hatago!" (the quarter of Edo where Yagorō lived), and when the actors left the stage at the end of the play they were encouraged by shouts of, "Thanks for your trouble!" The spectators directed comments not only at the actors but at the gentry upstairs. No matter how interesting the Nō or Kyōgen in progress, the arrivals and departures of ladies of quality were greeted with a barrage of wisecracks, sometimes of a decidedly improper nature. A contemporary account relates, "The tumult inside the theatre was indescribable. Everyone was making so much noise all at once that it was impossible to understand what was being said." Clearly, the audience was enjoying not only the plays but the rare opportunity to give vent to their high spirits in the presence of the grandees of the country. The actors no doubt found it a strain to perform before such spectators, but they endured the discomfort, remembering that the purpose of the benefit performances was to make money. In this they succeeded admirably. Enterprising merchants also seized the opportunity to profit by the crowds; concessions were given out for tea, saké, *sushi*, cushions, and even for the disposal of waste matter in the public toilets. Hōshō Yagorō earned twenty thousand *ryō*, and the government itself considered the event of such importance that the reign-name was changed to Kaei ("celebration of eternity") in commemoration.

The benefit performances each day consisted of *Okina*, one Nō from each of the five categories, a final, congratulatory Nō, and five Kyōgen. Hōshō Kurō, who was to emerge as the leading actor of the Meiji period, appeared as the *shite* on each day of the series, though only a boy of eleven in

1848. He succeeded as head of the school in 1853, the year that Commodore Perry's ships arrived off Edo, and performed at New Year both in 1854 for the Shogun Ieshige and in 1858 for his successor Iemochi. These were the last command performances of the shogunate, though Hōshō Kurō continued until 1861 to appear occasionally on the stage inside the castle.

MEIJI NŌ

Nō had been associated with the shogunate ever since the days of Yoshimitsu. With the overthrow of the shogunate in 1868 the actors were forced to decide whether to remain loyal to their old masters, now retired to Shizuoka, or to profess allegiance to the imperial government. Whichever course they might choose, there seemed little chance of ever performing again. Nō, like the Tokugawa régime which had so long supported it, was now in disgrace. Most actors gave up their profession, some to become farmers or shopkeepers, others to work with their hands. A few actors, notably Umewaka Minoru in Tokyo, struggled to preserve Nō. People were suspicious of Minoru, but he persisted, performing on a makeshift stage until he could secure a better one. Minoru with great difficulty persuaded Hōshō Kurō to revoke his decision of 1871 to retire from the stage and become a farmer. Kurō, an exceedingly cautious man who was hypersensitive about his dignity, finally consented in 1875 to appear on Minoru's stage when he realized that even under the new régime, with its passion for novelty and foreign things, there were still people capable of appreciating his art.

The subsequent revival of Nō, at a time when most old traditions were summarily rejected, was paradoxically due to the desire to emulate Western countries in offering suitably dignified entertainments on state occasions. The first performances of Nō after the Restoration were held in 1869 in honor of the visit of the Duke of Edinburgh. The Duke had to be entertained, but Kabuki was judged to be too vulgar for so exalted a guest, and Nō (despite its being in disgrace) was chosen instead. When Iwakura Tomomi, a court noble and high-ranking officer of the new government, visited Europe and America in 1871 he noticed similarities between Nō and opera, the usual entertainment provided state visitors abroad. A member of Iwakura's party commented, "I was never interested in Nō until I saw historical dramas abroad and thought how much they resembled Nō." The turning point in the modern history of Nō occurred on April 4, 1876, when the Emperor Meiji paid a visit to Iwakura Tomomi's residence and witnessed a program of Nō. Iwakura had decided, in the light of his experiences in Europe, that Nō was the appropriate entertainment to offer his sovereign. Performances for the Emperor were followed by another program intended for the Empress and the Empress Dowager, and a further program for the imperial princes and princesses. Umewaka Minoru, who had been entrusted with the performances, was able to find room for Hōshō Kurō in the program, though this had not originally been planned. His determination to draw Kurō back to the stage succeeded, and the collaboration of these two great actors made possible the revival of Nō.

The patronage of the imperial family protected Nō from any criticism of its association with the discredited shogunate. In the past, when the court was still in Kyoto, imperial approval had eagerly been sought by actors though it did not benefit them financially. The Emperor Kōmei, Meiji's father, had been especially fond of Nō and Kyōgen, but the actors who performed for him were rewarded not with robes or gifts of money, but with tastefully costumed little dolls. The Emperor Meiji's mother, the Empress Dowager Eishō (1833–1897), became after the Restoration the chief patron of Nō. In 1878 Meiji built for her pleasure a stage in the Aoyama Palace. Hōshō Kurō in later years described his experience at the inaugural performance: "I was to perform by command the difficult role of *Dōjōji*. The date for the opening had already been set when Ōkubo, the Minister of the Interior, was assassinated, and the inauguration of the stage was consequently delayed several times, finally being set for the fifth of July. I was in a state of extreme agitation for the weather was naturally very hot at that time of year and the role was demanding . . . When

I appeared on the stage I could see the Emperor's seat, but the heat and the demands of the role made me forget everything else. By the time I reached the *rambyōshi* section I had forgotten even the heat. At last came the interval, when I entered the bell. Once inside, I breathed a sigh of relief, only to begin feeling dizzy in the oppressive sultriness. I started to change my costume, wiping with a towel the waterfall of sweat pouring from me, when I discovered that someone had thoughtfully left a fan inside the bell. I used it to stir up a little breeze, put on my robes, turned myself into a serpent, and appeared once again on the stage." The performance, which lasted for nine hours, was judged an eminent success.

The visit of General Grant, the former President of the United States, in the summer of 1879 again provided an occasion for the presentation of Nō to a foreign visitor. Grant was the first head (or former head) of a foreign country ever to visit Japan, and the Japanese were understandably worried about how to entertain him. Grant, in the end, was treated to both Nō and Kabuki. At the conclusion of the Nō he witnessed at Iwakura's residence Grant is reported to have said, "So noble and beautiful an art is easily cheapened and destroyed by the changing tastes of the times. You must make efforts to preserve it." It is difficult to imagine the grizzled old soldier Grant being so powerfully impressed by the remote beauty of Nō, even with the assistance of the translation hastily prepared for the occasion, but his words were taken to heart by Iwakura, who decided that an organization was needed for the preservation of Nō. The Nō Society (*Nōgakusha*) which he founded built the first permanent Nō stage for the general public. In April, 1881, in the presence of the Empress Dowager and two hundred of the highest ranking nobles, the stage in Shiba Park was officially opened. On the third day, when the general public was admitted, over seven hundred persons attended. Umewaka Minoru's son (later known also as Umewaka Minoru) recollected his first stage appearance at the time, when he was four years old. "I was only a child and had no impressions worth mentioning, but I can still remember how beautiful everything seemed. On one side sat the Empress Dowager Eishō, her long hair hanging over her kimono, wearing a scarlet *hakama*, and with her were more than twenty court ladies, all in the same costume, sitting in a row. On the other side was the Empress Shōken. She and her attendants were all in Western costume, looking so beautiful they almost blinded me."

Public performances of Nō became frequent. The five schools, which had gladly appeared on the same stage in Shiba Park when their fortunes were low, before long found the financial support to build theatres for their exclusive use, and the differences between the various schools, which had not been so great as to prevent Umewaka Minoru of the Kanze school from appearing with Hōshō Kurō of the Hōshō school or Sakurama Bamba of the Komparu school, the third great actor of the period, from appearing on the Hōshō stage, were exaggerated. Rivalry over pupils, essential now that the government gave no direct support, further accentuated the differences. The Kanze school, the richest and most important, attracted a disproportionate number of students, perhaps sixty percent of the total, followed by Hōshō with another twenty percent or so; the remaining ten percent was divided among Komparu, Kongō and Kita, small schools whose existence at times has been threatened by the preference for more fashionable styles of Nō. Even the small schools, however, have produced outstanding performers such as Sakurama Kintarō (Komparu), Kongō Iwao (Kongō), and Kita Roppeita (Kita).

NŌ IN RECENT TIMES

The popularity of Nō continued to grow after the death or retirement of the great actors of the Meiji era, confounding the many prophets who had predicted that the younger generation would not respond to so outdated an art as Nō. Like other forms of traditional drama, Nō was favored by the wartime governments, anxious to foster belief in the importance of "pure" Japanese culture uncontaminated by foreign influences. New plays of a patriotic nature, like *Miikusabune* ("Imperial Warship") were composed and widely performed between 1942 and 1945, but quickly forgotten. Almost all the Nō stages in Tokyo were destroyed in 1945 by bombing, and for a time immediately afterwards all schools shared the one remaining stage, under conditions reminiscent of the early Meiji period. Renewed prosperity enabled most schools to build their own stages again.

Nō is today supported chiefly by people living in all parts of the country who study the singing, but not the performance, of the texts. The tuition fees they pay make it possible for Nō to be presented in the theatres, and when they visit Tokyo they naturally wish to see the plays they have learned by heart. We can judge how much they influence the programs from the fact that between 1949 and 1960 the Kanze school performed *Funa Benkei* 208 times and *Hagoromo* 193 times, though some masterpieces were seldom staged. *Teika* was performed only twenty-seven times, *Koi no Omoni* and *Eguchi* thirty-five times.

Performances by amateurs who have mastered the roles are also common and include some by women. Although no formal prohibition was placed on women appearing in Nō in the seventeenth century, when Kabuki was deprived of its actresses, they disappeared from the stage, and today people generally consider their voices and figures totally inadequate for even the most feminine roles. Nevertheless, women persist in their studies, and some day they may achieve recognition.

The study of Nō as a literary and theatrical art dates mainly from the Meiji period when such scholars as Yoshida Tōgo (1864–1918) discovered the texts of Zeami's criticism and other essential documents. Only since the 1930's, however, have truly scientific studies taken the place of the aimless compilation of facts or recollections which previously passed for criticism. The secrecy with which texts are still surrounded by some Nō masters has impeded basic research into the evolution of the texts, but this situation cannot long persist.

Performances today are at a high level. It is true that in some details the standards of the past cannot be equalled; for example, it has become prohibitively expensive to replace the covering of the drums for each performance, the practice in former days. Again, the actors' preference for the Western haircut means that sometimes in roles without masks they look incongruously modern. But these are minor flaws when compared to the devotion and scholarly attention which the roles receive. The reverent hush in the Nō theatre, as we have seen, is a relatively recent phenomenon. Certainly the manner of enjoying Nō must have been different when people brought food and drink to their boxes and divided their attention between the stage and their stomachs. Some today regret the changes, recalling wistfully easier-going days, but artistically they would seem to be in the right direction, pointing to a return to the ideals of Zeami and, indeed, to the solemn beginnings of Nō.

III. NŌ AND KYŌGEN AS LITERATURE

THE TEXTS of the Nō plays have often been likened to brocade woven of brilliant bits of silk to form a magnificent fabric, a simile which suggests how liberally the texts were embellished with scraps from the literature of the past. The *tanka*, the classic verse form, in particular gave the poetry of Nō its distinctive tone. Ever since the tenth century, when the anthology *Kokinshū* ("Collection of Ancient and Modern Poetry") was compiled, the *tanka* had been revered as the noblest form of Japanese poetry, and a thorough knowledge of the *tanka* in the dozen imperial anthologies was assumed of educated men. Zeami urged aspiring Nō actors not to dissipate their talents on other arts, but he made an exception for the *tanka*, the source of so much beauty in the Nō.

The *tanka* had even been credited with supernatural powers. The preface to the *Kokinshū* asserts that the *tanka* can move the gods and demons. We find echoes of this belief in the plays. The central theme of *Shiga* is that the *tanka* promotes the security and happiness of the people because it enjoys the protection of the gods and Buddhas. In *Utaura* a knowledge of the *tanka* is declared to be a means of knowing the future, for poetry reflects the minds of the gods. Zeami often quoted famous *tanka*, sometimes a whole poem, sometimes only a verse or two, confident that his audience would catch the allusions. Quotation of the old *tanka* not only confirmed the mood of a scene by its reference to similar feelings described in the past, but enhanced the text with the magical aura of divinely-favored words.

The bits of silk making up the brocade of the texts did not consist entirely of *tanka*. The play *Atsumori*, for example, quotes not only four *tanka* but phrases from the preface to *Kokinshū*, poems in Chinese by Po Chü-i and others, Buddhist works, *The Tale of Genji* and, above all, *The Tale of the Heike*, the thirteenth-century novel which inspired the play. The number of quotations should not suggest that *Atsumori* is a mere tissue of allusions, a pastiche composed of famous tags from the old classics. Only a small part of the text can be traced to earlier literature, and even these borrowings usually consist of a few key words rather than extended passages. The texts are original works given added depth and complexity by the use of quotations and allusions.

Zeami in his critical writings was concerned mainly with analysis of the art of acting, but he also mentioned on occasion his conviction that the texts themselves were of paramount importance. Unquestionably he took enormous pains with the literary effects of his plays. Zeami's style is marked not only by his reliance on quotations from literary works but by extraordinary complexity in the expression, far beyond the requirements of the theatre. Zeami's use of wordplays, especially the *kakekotoba* or "pivot word," which shifts in meaning depending on the words preceding and following, was another aspect of his constant attempt to supply additional layers of meaning to his words. Zeami did not invent the *kakekotoba*, but he used it with greater effect than any of his predecessors. This passage from *Hanjo* by Zeami contains four *kakekotoba*:

YOSHIDA: *konata ni mo*   I too have a keepsake

     wasuregatami no   Impossible to forget:

	koto no ha wo	The words we spoke.
	Iwade *no mori no*	But if, like azaleas hidden
	shita tsutsuji	In the silent wood of Iwade,
	iro ni idezu wa	You do not speak,
	sore zo to mo	You show nothing in your face,
	mite koso shirame	How am I to understand?
	kono ōgi	Seeing it, I shall know:
		Your fan.
HANJO:	mite wa sate	Seeing it?
	nani no tame zo to	What use would that be?
	yūgure no	What good can it do
	tsuki wo idaseru	Importuning me so
	ōgi no e no	For a fan with a picture
	kaku *bakari*	Painted to reveal
	nani no tame naruran	The twilight moon?

In this passage Yoshida asks the courtesan Hanjo for the fan he gave her as a pledge of his love, a fan showing the moon at twilight. The translation resorts to double meanings for the *kakekotoba*, but it is unfortunately impossible to suggest in English the force of the Japanese puns. *Wasuregata* means "difficult to forget" with the preceding phrase, but the added syllable *mi* yields another word *katami* ("keepsake") when used with the next phrase. Similarly, *iwade* with the preceding phrase means "not speaking," but with the following phrase is the proper noun Iwade, the name of a forest. *Yū* means "to say," but the suffix *gure* forms the word *yūgure* (twilight). *Kaku* means "to paint" but also "so." Each wordplay enriches the texture with relevant meanings, and affords a compression parallel to the economy of the Nō theatre itself; it is like a magnificently attired actor moving in intricate patterns against the starkly austere setting.

Another feature of Zeami's style is his use of *engo*, or "related words." *Engo* are words chosen from among possible synonyms for their overtones, with the intent of creating a unity of echoes even when the surface meanings are seemingly unrelated. A similar use of language can be found, say, in the thirtieth sonnet of Shakespeare:

> When to the *sessions* of sweet silent thought
> I *summon* up remembrance of things past . . .

Although the main theme is grief over the passage of time, the pervading echoes are those of the courtroom. In Nō the underlying imagery may give a unity to the text: in *Hachinoki* the dominant images are related to snow and purity; in *Obasute* to the moon; in *Eguchi* to a river. The use of this unifying imagery makes it far easier for the Nō actor, with the limited means of representation at his disposal, to project the essential mood of a play.

The most impressive feature of Zeami's style is the power of the imagery. The art of Nō demands a transformation of violent and jagged emotions into a prescribed, unruffled form. In this respect it may remind us of the tragedies of Racine; the surface elegance is broken only occasionally, but those moments stand out with electrifying intensity. Zeami's most powerful work, *Kinuta*, is dominated by the hollow sound of clothes being beaten on a fulling block, evoking the loneliness of long autumn nights. The woman in the play, incensed at her husband's failure to return to her, calls for a fulling block on which to pound out her grief:

inga no mōshū	Tears of remembrance
omoi no namida	For sins committed
kinuta ni kakareba	Fall on the fulling block;
namida wa kaette	The tears turn to flames,
kaen to natte	And choked by the smoke

mune no kemuri no	Of the fire in my breast,
honō ni musebeba	I shriek, but my voice
sakedo koe ga	Does not escape my lips.
ideba koso	The fulling block is soundless,
kinuta mo koe naku	The pine wind too, unheard . . .
matsukaze mo kikoezu	Only the shouts of hell's tormentors,
kashaku no koe no mi	Horrible their cries!
osoroshiya	

In this passage Zeami used with superb effect the Buddhist terms *inga* ("cause and effect"), *mōshū* ("deep-rooted delusion"), *kaen* ("flames"), and *kashaku* ("tormentors"), words that not only possess powerful religious overtones but by their very sounds, unlike the softer syllables of pure Japanese, give sharp contours to the lines. The intensity of the imagery—tears that turn into flames, mute shrieks of anguish, the cries of the fiends of hell—imprints the passage with the controlled violence of Nō at its most dramatic.

A whole play could not, of course, be maintained at this level. Sections are in prose, declaimed in a conventionally stylized manner; most sentences end with the mournfully prolonged vowels of the copula verb *sōrō*. Other sections, though in poetry, are in a low key, conforming to the prescription that the *jo* section of a play be slow and serene. The structural requirements of the plays, as established by Zeami himself, also tend to confine the poetry of greatest intensity to a few sections, generally at the close of the *ha* division of the work.

An analysis of a typical play of the *waki* (first) category, *Takasago*, by Zeami, may illustrate the structure and the uses of different kinds of poetry.

The play opens as the *waki*, a Shinto priest, embarks with his companions on a journey. They sing the *shidai*, a passage in three lines of 7+5, 7+5, and 7+4 syllables, the first two lines being identical:

ima wo hajime no	*tabigoromo*	Now first we wear our travel robes,
ima wo hajime no	*tabigoromo*	Now first we wear our travel robes,
hi mo yuku sue zo	*hisashiki*	How long are the days of travel ahead.

After singing this passage the *waki* speaks the *nanori*, a passage in prose identifying himself, and relates his intention of making a journey. He and his companions now sing the *michiyuki* (travel song) in seven or eight lines of 5, 7+5 syllables, etc., ending with the statement of their arrival at Takasago. The poetry is in the restrained tone appropriate to the *jo* section, which concludes at this point.

The *ha* section opens with the appearance of the *shite* and *tsure*, an old man and an old woman. Their entrance song, known as the *issei*, consists of lines in 5, 7+5, and 7+5 syllables.

takasago no		At Takasago
matsu no harukaze	*fukikurete*	A spring breeze in the pines blows as dusk falls,
onoe no kane mo	*hibiku naru*	And the temple bell on the peak echoes the close of day.

Next come passages known as *ninoku* (second stanza) and *sannoku* (third stanza), each a line in 7+5 syllables:

nami wa kasumi no	*isogakure*	The waves are hidden at the misty beach,
oto koso shio no	*michihi nare*	Their sound tells of the ebb and flow of the tide.

The scene having been set, the *shite* describes his situation in the *sashi*, usually a passage in about ten lines of 7+5 syllables each:

tare wo ka mo	Whom shall I take

shiru hito ni sen takasago no	As my friend? Even the pine
matsu mo mukashi no tomo narade	Of Takasago is not a friend of old;
sugikoshi yo yo wa shirayuki no	The years on years I have lived through
	are forgotten, but the snows
tsumori tsumorite oi no tsuru no	Keep piling, piling; the aged crane
negura ni nokoru ariyake no	In his nest, a spring moon lingering
haru no shimoyo no okii ni mo	In the frosty dawn, awakens:
matsukaze wo no mi kikinarete	I hear nothing but the familiar pine wind,
kokoro wo tomo to sugamushiro	But making its song my friend, as I lie
	on my rush mat,
omoi wo noburu bakari nari	I tell my griefs, my only solace.

Apart from the extra line in five syllables, a common variation, this *sashi* is quite regular. But what complications are involved in the poetry! The passage opens with a *tanka* from an imperial collection, quoted in a slightly altered form: "Whom shall I make my friend? Even the pine of Takasago is not a friend of old." The next line contains a *kakekotoba*, *shirayuki*, meaning "I do not know" (or "do not remember") with what precedes, but "white snow" with the following words *tsumori tsumorite* ("piling, piling"), alluding to the white hair of the speaker, so old that he no longer has any friends and has even forgotten the past. "The aged crane" is used metaphorically for an old person, but leads also to "nest." These different images coalesce: piled-up snow lies in the nest of the aged crane; the aged crane wakes in a nest lit by the moon lingering in the frosty sky of a spring dawn; the crane becomes a metaphor for the old man who, wakening at night, hears the wind through the pines and makes this poetic sound his friend; and finally, the old man is comforted by expressing his grief in poetry.

Granted that some in the audience could follow these complexities, most spectators probably caught no more than the general drift. The clusters of images, blending imprecisely in their minds, produced an impression of beauty.

Takasago is a calmly majestic play, suitable to the category of god plays. The *sashi*, which occurs at the opening of the *ha* section, was not the place for displaying powerful emotions; nevertheless, Zeami's poetry builds a gradual intensification of interest. The first part of the *ha* section concludes with the singing of the *sageuta* (three or four lines of 5, 7+5, 7+5 syllables) and the *ageuta* (up to ten units of 7+5 syllables). At this point the *shite* encounters the *waki* for the first time.

The second part of the *ha* section begins with exchanges of dialogue in prose between the *shite* and *waki* about the Takasago Pine. The prose rises into poetry that continues the dialogue. Now the chorus enters for the first time, singing a passage in nine lines. This *ageuta*, often sung on auspicious occasions, begins:

shikai nami shizuka ni te	The waves of the four seas are calm,
kuni mo osamaru toki tsu kaze	The land at peace; favorable winds
eda wo narasanu mi yo nareya	Disturb not the branches in this holy era . . .

The third part of the *ha* section, the central episode of the whole play, describes the glory of pines and of poetry. It begins with the *kuri*, a short passage in no fixed meter. A *sashi* follows, also in free rhythms, and then the *kuse*, a long section describing how each sight of nature inspires poetry. All three passages are sung by the chorus with occasional interpellations from the *shite*. The irregularity of the meter reflects the importance of the music and dance in this part.

The *kuse* is followed by the *rongi*, a dialogue between chorus and *shite* in regular meter, terminating with the *shite*'s departure from the stage. A Kyōgen actor, identified as "a man of the place," appears, and after a few brief exchanges with the *waki*, recites the history of the Pine of Takasago. In some plays the *ai* section merely repeats in simpler language information already given; probably it was necessary for spectators who failed to understand the plot from the difficult sung passages.

After the *ai* is completed, the *kyū* section of the play begins. Usually this occupies only a page or two in print, but in performance it often takes twenty or more minutes mainly because it contains the final dance of the *shite*. The *kyū* section usually (but not in *Takasago*) begins with the *waki*'s song of waiting, seven or eight lines in 5, 7+5, 7+5 meter, followed by the second appearance of the *shite* to a *sashi* of three lines in 5, 7+5, 7+5 syllables. In *Takasago* the *shite* reveals himself as being in reality the god of the Sumiyoshi Shrine. Next ensues a dialogue between *shite* and chorus on the miraculous nature of the god, followed by the *shimai*, the final dance. A last *rongi* (dialogue) between *shite* and chorus, generally in about fifteen lines, ends most plays; in *Takasago* it is an expression of awe and delight over the revelation of the god Sumiyoshi.

Hardly a single play fits this formula exactly. Zeami himself cited *Yumi Yawata* as a model work, attributing its regularity to its sacred character. But even though the elements of most plays are somewhat at variance with the ideal pattern, perhaps to avoid monotony, their overall construction generally corresponds closely to that of *Takasago*.

Plays of the first category are the least rewarding dramatically. *Takasago* is one of the most interesting examples; a more typical work, like *Shirahige*, requires the *shite* to sit motionless in the middle of the stage through most of the performance as the chorus recites events associated with a shrine.

Plays of the second category, the warrior plays, are distinctly more dramatic. Because they belong to the slow section of the program, they do not approach the violence or emotional intensity of plays about warriors presented later in the program; of the sixteen *shuramono* (warrior plays) in the current repertory, thirteen are by Zeami, a sure indication that these plays are more likely to be poetic than realistic depictions of martial deeds.

Many warrior plays were derived from *The Tale of the Heike*, that repository of stirring or pathetic incidents from the wars between the Taira and the Minamoto. Zeami declared in his critical writings that texts based on this work must be faithful to the original, but his own are free, not only in language but in emphasis. *Atsumori*, for example, retains little of the original dramatic tension; the source is in fact more theatrical than the play. In *The Tale of the Heike* we are told how the Minamoto captain Kumagai challenges a fleeing enemy general to an encounter. They fight, and Kumagai fells his opponent. Tearing off the man's helmet, he discovers a boy of sixteen, a noble, and decides to spare his life, remembering how grieved he had been that day when his own son, also sixteen, was wounded. In polite, almost deferential language, Kumagai asks the boy his name, but the boy insolently recommends that Kumagai show his severed head to men on his side. The superbly dramatic dialogue is broken by the approach of other Minamoto soldiers. Kumagai, resigned now to killing Atsumori, the young man, promises to pray for his repose. He kills the boy and strips his armor, only to find a flute, a further reminder of the boy's aristocratic lineage. In the end Kumagai abandons his career as a soldier to become a priest.

In the play *Atsumori*, Kumagai appears as the *waki*, the priest Renshō. He tells of his intention to pray for Atsumori's repose at Ichinotani, the site of the Heike defeat. There he encounters some reapers and hears one play a flute. This reaper remains after the others go and tells the priest that he is of Atsumori's family. After the interlude the young man reappears as a ghost in armor, this time identifying himself as Atsumori. He relates the disasters that struck the Taira family, and recalls how he played his flute the night before the battle. Finally he relives his mortal struggle with Kumagai, but at the moment that he raises his sword to strike, in the gesture of a *shura*, a still resentful ghost, he sees that the priest Renshō is praying for his salvation. "Pray for me again, oh, pray for me again," are the concluding words of the play.

Comparing the two stories we see that almost every element of pathos or drama in *The Tale of the Heike* has been deleted from the play. Atsumori's youth, his resemblance to Kumagai's son, his insolence in response to Kumagai's solicitude, Kumagai's regret when forced to kill Atsumori— all are eliminated, leaving only the story of a man unable to forget his defeat at an enemy's hands.

Of course, the audience was familiar with the story as told in *The Tale of the Heike*, but Zeami's play does not depend on this knowledge; instead, he chose to delete everything particular about the two men in the interests of achieving a stylized, universal tragedy. One man kills another; by this act he brings salvation to both. Kumagai's remorse over killing Atsumori leads to his taking Buddhist orders, and this act in turn ultimately brings Atsumori salvation. The attention of the author of *The Tale of the Heike* was focused on the dramatic contrasts between the two men: the grizzled warrior and the boy-soldier, the rough frontiersman and the flute-playing aristocrat, the compassionate old man and the insolent youth. In the play, however, the central theme is Atsumori's release from the torment of being a *shura*. His ghost has lingered on earth in the guise of a reaper because, unable to attain salvation, his attachment to the world makes him relive again and again the moments of his final battle. Only his flute, the symbol of his youth and noble aspirations, brings solace to this tortured spirit. When Renshō promises the unknown reaper to pray for his soul, Atsumori appears in his true form. He repeats the motions of his mortal encounter with Kumagai, raising his sword with the cry, "Here is my enemy!" But at that moment he is saved. He cries, "We shall be reborn on the same lotus!"

Zeami chose not to dwell on the contrasts found in *The Tale of the Heike*. Atsumori's inability to renounce his memories of this world does not stem from his youth, his courtly accomplishments or his pride; only when he recognizes that Renshō is not his enemy can he be saved. The play, though telling of warriors, neither glorifies nor condemns the military life. Zeami wrote that plays dealing with soldiers of the Heike wars must be elegant: "In plays of this type especially, a brilliance of effect is desirable." In *Atsumori* the boy's youthful beauty and the music of his flute impart *yūgen*, as in *Tsunemasa* the music of the *biwa* or in *Tadanori* the cherry blossoms on the strand of Suma give a haunting beauty to the stories of defeated warriors. The more powerful *Kanehira*, on the other hand, has little of this quality:

hakujin hone wo	Horror of naked blades
kudaku kurushimi	Smashing on bone,
gansei wo yaburi	Scenes of eyes gouged out,
kōha tate wo nagasu yosōi	And shields floating on crimson waves
yanagui ni	Like scattered blossoms
zanka wo midasu	Breaking against a weir.*

Kanehira belongs to the world of the *shura;* the characters are proud of their hours of glory and need no priest to pray for their salvation. *Kanehira* is more exciting than *Atsumori*, but it fits poorly into the *jo* section of a program, and its lack of *yūgen* suggests that Zeami, despite traditional attributions, was not the author.

Plays of the third category, the woman plays, contain the most beautiful poetry. Love, when treated in this category, has a bittersweet fragrance, though apt in plays of the fourth category to be an obsession powerful enough to derange a woman. The story of Lady Rokujō, derived from *The Tale of Genji*, is described touchingly in the third-category play *Nonomiya*, where we see her at a lonely shrine in the fields awaiting her last meeting with Genji; in the fourth-category play *Aoi no Ue*, Rokujō's love for Genji is depicted as the demonic instrument of the death of Aoi, Genji's wife. The poetry in each case creates the mood. In *Nonomiya* we find:

nonomiya no	My carriage is bright
aki no chigusa no	With the thousand autumn grasses
hanaguruma	Of the Shrine in the Fields.
ware mo mukashi ni	The wheels turn; I too
meguri kinikeri	Have returned to the past.

The hollow sound of the drum accompanying the poetry suggests with unspeakable pathos the autumn, season of memories. When Rokujō, passing under the *torii*, the boundary between life

*Translation by Stanleigh H. Jones, Jr. in Keene, *Twenty Plays of the Nō Theatre*, p. 275.

and death, disappears, perhaps at last to gain release from the love of Genji which binds her still to the world of the living, we sense almost painfully the lonely, mysterious beauty of *yūgen*:

nonomiya no	Even the moon
tsuki mo mukashi ya	At the Shrine in the Fields
omouran	Must remember the past;
kage samishiku mo	Its light forlornly trickles
mori no shitatsuyu	Through the leaves to the forest dew,
mori no shitatsuyu	Through the leaves to the forest dew.
mi no okidokoro mo	This place, once my refuge,
aware mukashi no	This garden, still lingers
niwa no tatazumai	Unchanged from long ago,
yoso ni zo kawaru	A beauty nowhere else,
keshiki mo kari naru	Though transient, insubstantial
koshibagaki	As this little wooden fence
tsuyu uchiharai	From which he used to brush the dew.
towareshi ware mo	I, whom he visited,
sono hito mo	And he, my lover too,
tada yume no yo to	The whole world turned to dreams,
furiyuku ato ni	To aging ruins;
tare matsu	Whom should I pine for now?
mushi no ne wa	The voices of pine-crickets
rin rin toshite	Trill *rin*, *rin*,
kaze bōbō taru	The wind howls:
nonomiya no yosugara	How I remember
natsukashiya	Nights at the Shrine in the Fields!

The sin of attachment, which draws ghosts back to memories they cannot relinquish, is most affectingly evoked in the woman plays, where the memories are not of vengeance, but of love. In *Izutsu*, Ariwara no Narihira's childhood sweetheart recalls their early happiness together, contrasting those days with his later deceit. She puts on Narihira's court robe and cap and, going to the well-curb *(izutsu)* where as children she and Narihira compared heights, looks at her reflection in the water.

mireba natsukashiya	She looks—how sweet the memory,
warenagara natsukashiya	Sweet the memory, though of herself,
bōfū hakurei no sugata wa	This ghost in her dead husband's form:
shibomeru hana no	A withered flower,
iro nōte	Color vanished,
nioi nokorite	Perfume only lingering.
Ariwara no tera no kane mo	The bell of the Ariwara Temple too
honobono to akureba	Tolls dimly in the dawning.
furudera no	Over the old temple,
matsukaze ya	The wind through the pines,
bashōba no	The rustle of plantain leaves,
yume mo yaburete	Broken easily as dreams;
samenikeri	Awakened,
yume wa yabure	The dream is broken,
akenikeri	The day has dawned.

The texts are replete with ingenuity—plays on words, thoughts that shift in direction, sounds echoed from one line to the next, adjectives modifying both the word they follow and the word they precede—but they do not represent virtuosity for its own sake; the complexity should suggest the shifting flow of thoughts of the characters themselves. The poignancy achieved in the poetry, rather than any display of femininity in performance, gives the woman plays their heart-breaking beauty.

The fourth category includes the widest variety of works, ranging from plays hardly distinguishable from the poetic dramas of the third category to realistic plays almost devoid of poetry. *Hagoromo*, which tells of a goddess who must perform a celestial dance as the price of a fisherman's returning her robe of feathers, is sometimes classed in the fourth category, presumably because the presence of the fisherman lends a realistic note, but it by no means resembles the bulk of the *genzaimono*, or contemporary plays. *Jinen Koji* by Kannami, an early *genzaimono*, tells of a girl who has sold herself to white slavers so that she can make an offering to the memory of her dead parents. The priest Jinen Koji, discovering what has happened, rushes after her, arriving at the shore of Lake Biwa just as the men are rowing off their boat, with the girl lying in the bottom, bound and gagged. Jinen induces the men to return the girl, but in exchange they demand that he perform the songs and dances for which he is famous. The one thing common to *Hagoromo* and *Jinen Koji* (and to many other plays of the fourth category) is that the dances are identified in the play as such, and are not heightened, abstract expressions of the emotions described in the poetry.

Another important group of plays belonging to the fourth category are those dealing with mad persons. "Madness," however, is by no means uncontrolled lunacy; it embraces such emotions as the overpowering grief of the mother in *Sumidagawa* who searches the country for her kidnapped child, or the jealous despair of the woman in *Kinuta* who fears that her husband has deserted her. These women are obsessed rather than mad, but "madness" in Zeami's day, like the divine madness of the Greeks, was associated with poetry and music; the other characters in *Sumidagawa* ask the distraught mother to display her madness, as if excess of grief had made her entertaining.

Plays of the fourth category usually recount a story rather than attempt to create a poetic atmosphere. Audiences have always responded more readily to such works than to those of more remote beauty, and as a group they are highly popular. *Aoi no Ue*, *Hachinoki*, *Dōjōji*, *Ataka* and *Sumidagawa*, though entirely dissimilar in mood and plot, all engage the audience less by their beauty of language than by their theatrical effectiveness. Yet for all their comparative theatricality, they are far removed, say, from Kabuki. The plot of *Ataka* is virtually identical to that of the Kabuki play *Kanjinchō*, but it remains stylized and aloof where *Kanjinchō* is warmly human; nothing in *Ataka* has the quality of the touching moment in *Kanjinchō* when Yoshitsune, aware how painful it must have been for Benkei to strike him, his master, extends his hand towards Benkei in a gesture of affection and understanding. However dramatic a Nō play may be, its symbolic possibilities can be preserved only if a distance is kept between the play and the audience. An unadorned play like *Shunnei* is likely to drop from the repertory even if its plot is interesting.

The final components of a Nō program, the devil plays, are closely related to those of the fourth category, but their tempo is faster, as we should expect in the *kyū* section. The *shite* is often a demonic being who appears in the second part wearing an enormous red or white wig that cascades over his brilliant costume, and the frenzied movements of his dance are accentuated by the ferocity of his mask. The props too, unlike the customary bare outlines of a house, tree or gate, may be solidly constructed platforms ornamented with gold and silver trees. In the first part of these plays the *shite* is likely to appear in some pleasant guise—as a gentlewoman in *Momijigari*, a priest in *Tsuchigumo*, or an old woman in *Kurozuka*—but in the second part the demon reveals his true form, and stamps wildly, swinging a mallet. The lively tempo of the play creates a cheerful impression on the audience, despite the frightening presence of a demon, and brings the program to a satisfying close.

The demon plays were written mainly by playwrights of the century after Zeami. Though effective as theatre and sometimes moving as poetry, they fail to touch the exalted utterance of the greatest Nō plays. It has been said of *Funa Benkei*, nevertheless, that "of the two hundred works in the current repertory, it ranks as a masterpiece of the kind one can count on the fingers of one hand." It rates this praise especially because of its brilliant variety of effects. In the first scene Benkei persuades Yoshitsune to dismiss his sweetheart Shizuka, who has accompanied him on the flight from the capital. The actor playing Shizuka must suggest the grief of this ill-starred woman; but in the second scene the same actor, taking an entirely different part, must rage with masculine vigor as Tomomori, a defeated Heike warrior who rises from the sea to menace the fugitives in their boat. Between the two sections of the play an unusually absorbing *ai-kyōgen* is played by the boatman who ferries Yoshitsune, Benkei and the others across the Inland Sea. He battles with tremendous waves stirred up by Tomomori's ghost, giving vent to realistic cries and gestures that contrast with the stylization of the rest of the play.

The demands of sixteenth-century audiences for action and lively presentation probably account for such works as *Shōzon*, *Chikatō* and *Kasui* by Nagatoshi. The former two works each have nine characters, *Kasui* has thirteen. *Shōzon*, the tale of a plot against Yoshitsune's life thwarted by Benkei, is devoid of poetry, and is performed by some schools with such acrobatics as somersaults and perpendicular backward falls. *Chikatō* has four principal characters, each given a display scene, rather in the manner of an Italian opera. *Kasui*, a work not currently performed, has many changes of scene, and its plot shifts from the fable of a dragon princess who dries up a river in order to compel the Chinese court to provide her with a husband, to the more realistic scene of the courtier who volunteers to marry her, to a strange episode in which a great drum sounds of itself, presaging war, and finally to a battle scene in which the Chinese emperor, aided by the Dragon King, is victorious. The dances in these plays are no longer natural outgrowths of the poetry but arbitrary insertions, and the texts themselves are as conventional as they are flat. *Hatsuyuki* by Zempō, more poetic than most plays of the period, contains these uninspiring lines:

are are miyo ya	Oh, oh, just look!
fushigi ya na	How strange it is!
are are miyo ya	Oh, oh, just look!
fushigi ya na	How strange it is!
nakazora no kumo ka to	What seemed to be
mietsuru ga	A cloud high in the sky
kumo ni wa arade	Is not a cloud:
samo shirotae no	White as glossy silk,
Hatsuyuki no	Hatsuyuki,
tsubasa wo tarete	Lowering its wings,
tobikitari	Has flown back.
himegimi ni mukai	Its form as it dances,
samo natsukashige ni	Ever so affectionately,
tachimau sugata	Facing the princess,
ge ni aware naru	Makes a truly touching
keshiki ka na	Sight to behold.

The plays by Nagatoshi and Zempō mark the end of the creative period of Nō. It should be noted, however, that many plays are of unknown authorship, and we cannot even assign them an approximate date. *Nonomiya*, *Hagoromo*, *Utō*, *Kumasaka*, *Yuya*, *Kantan*, *Tsuchigumo*, *Hachinoki* and *Kagekiyo* are among the plays which traditionally were ascribed to Zeami but now, in the absence of firm evidence of authorship, are listed as "other works." But if *Nonomiya*, *Yuya* and the rest were actually by another dramatist, he surely ranks (despite his anonymity) as Zeami's equal. It seems improbable that so great a genius could have remained completely unknown. It may be that the reaction against unproved attributions has been excessive, and future discoveries will enable us to credit Zeami with masterpieces whose authorship is now uncertain. His genius was not likely to have occurred twice.

KYŌGEN

The name Kyōgen, written with characters meaning "wild words," seems to have originated in a Chinese phrase which derogatively described all literature as being no more than "wild words and fancy language." The phrase came to be used in a Buddhist sense, with the implication that even frivolous writings may provide the impetus to salvation. It figures in some plays as a designation for the art of Nō itself. In *Tōgan Koji* the lines occur, "One can enter the true path of giving praise to the Buddha and setting the wheel of his Law in motion by means of 'wild words and fancy language.' Let us celebrate this flower of the human heart." The farcical Kyōgen plays may have been dignified as being a path that leads to enlightenment in order to justify their innocent frivolity.

By Zeami's day both *ai* and independent Kyōgen formed part of Nō programs. Zeami mentions that performances offered at shrines customarily included three Nō and two Kyōgen. The alternation of Nō and Kyōgen became the general rule. Kyōgen actors, in addition to appearing in *ai* and in the farces themselves, performed in Nō, usually in minor roles, as servants, messengers and the like. Generally the dialogue for these parts consists merely of such phrases as "I obey your commands," but occasionally, as in *Hanjo* (where the brothel proprietress is performed by a Kyōgen actor) the roles have dramatic importance.

The different functions of Kyōgen actors on the Nō stage indicate how intimately the two arts were related. Kyōgen, however, was normally considered only a minor element in the program. Zeami's prescription for Kyōgen actors suggests he held them in low esteem: "A Kyōgen actor performing in the *ai-kyōgen* of a Nō play should refrain from attempting to make the audience laugh. His function is to relate the plot of the Nō and to address himself to the audience in such a way that they will feel he has actually seen and heard the events he describes."

The subordinate position of Kyōgen is further suggested by the fact that the texts were not recorded until the beginning of the seventeenth century. The first substantial collection, published in 1660 under the name *Kyōgenki*, included fifty plays. This edition and a much augmented later version are now dismissed as being mere explanations of the plots with snatches of dialogue, and not accurate transcriptions of the texts. But though inferior and misleading, these are the oldest versions we have; a 1578 collection, the earliest Kyōgen document, consists merely of brief summaries. The lack of authentic texts dating back to the sixteenth century forces us to depend on the oral traditions of the three schools—Ōkura, Izumi, and the now defunct Sagi. In principle, each Kyōgen teacher carefully transmits the texts word-by-word to his pupils, but minor variants exist even within a single school, and a comparison of the texts of the three schools reveals enormous differences, not only in the dialogue but even in the structure of the plays. Probably these variants are very old: the bare outlines of the plot may originally have been the actors' only guide, the dialogue being left largely to improvisation. For this reason it is foolish to search for authors of the plays. Undoubtedly someone, whether an actor or a dramatist, first conceived the plots, but the lines developed naturally over the years, successful passages being retained and others dropped, rather than originating like Nō in a single writer's imagination.

The Kyōgen plays vary so markedly in literary quality that some scholars believe it is possible to trace a progression from early, unsophisticated works to the later masterpieces. The oldest Kyōgen were probably in the tradition of *Okina*, festive plays depicting the villagers' hopes for a prosperous new year. *Sannimpu* ("The Three Farmers"), for example, describes the happy journey of the three farmers to the capital in order to pay their taxes, no hardship in a year of peace and plenty. Such works contain more singing and dancing than the more satirical Kyōgen, and the humorous elements are minor. Congratulatory Kyōgen are sometimes referred to as *waki* Kyōgen, by analogy to the *waki* Nō, because they are presented first in a program.

The later Kyōgen are marked by greater ingenuity of plot, cleverer situations and a sharp decrease in musical or choreographic elements. The parts are often referred to as the *shite* (or *omo*) and *ado*, corresponding to the *shite* and *waki* of Nō, but there is little subordination of one part to the other; in a play like *Shūron* where a priest of the Amida sect and a priest of the Nichiren sect try to outsmart each other, it is essential that they be equal antagonists. Though secondary characters tend to be stereotypes with little individuality, they certainly assert themselves far more vigorously than the *waki* or *tsure* of Nō. As dramas the Kyōgen are therefore closer to Western theatre than most Nō plays; in recent years a few medieval European farces have even been adapted to the Kyōgen stage. The later Kyōgen partake of the universal nature of farce, though never descending to the crudities typical of many Western examples. They lack the refined wit of high comedy, but they afford the actors maximum opportunities to display ringing voices and agile bodily movements.

A Kyōgen actor may appear in any part, regardless of his age, physical appearance or voice, but some prefer the part of Tarōkaja (the servant), others the termagant wife, and still others the more pathetic roles. Most parts are performed without either masks or makeup. An actor taking the part of a woman merely ties a towel around his head in an approximation of a female head-dress, but neither in voice nor in movements does he suggest femininity. Child actors may perform not only as children but in roles of indeterminate age; their high-pitched monotones do scant justice to the lines, but the childish gravity they display in reciting and dancing endears them to the audience.

Masks are used chiefly when actors appear as non-human beings—animals, demons or gods— but there are also comically ugly masks for both male and female roles. Unlike Nō, where the mask may represent the "true" appearance of the characters, Kyōgen masks are often put on as a means of deception; a character may pretend to be a god (as in *Ishigami*) or a demon (as in *Oba ga Sake*) in order to frighten another person into obeying his wishes. Masks are used only in about one-eighth of the plays of the Kyōgen repertory.

The style of the Kyōgen texts is infinitely less complicated (and less distinguished) than that of Nō. Except for occasional songs, sometimes in mock imitation of Nō, the texts are in prose, each sentence generally ending with the copula verb *gozaru*. Whole passages may be the same from play to play, and there is much repetition in the dialogue. Audiences are not bored with such repetitions; on the contrary, they provide pleasingly familiar elements close to the essence of Kyōgen. The daimyo, for example, usually summons his servant Tarōkaja with the words: *Yai, yai, yai, Tarōkaja, oru ka yai?* The translation, "Hey, Tarōkaja, are you there?" certainly gives no idea of the effect of the Japanese. Translation is even more inadequate when it comes to Tarō-kaja's response, a long *Haaaaaah*, rising about two octaves, and translatable only as "Yes."

Kyōgen possesses little of the literary merit of its tragic counterpart, Nō. It occupies a position somewhere between a comedy of masks and true comedy, but relies most heavily for its effects not on the texts but on the manner of presentation—the intonation, the stylized movements of the actors, and the delightful cadences of the sentences ending in *gozaru*. A few of the plays boast plots ingenious enough to survive even in translation, and many others are enjoyable because of the glimpses they afford into the lives of the common people of the sixteenth and seventeenth centuries, but Kyōgen needs a stage for even a fraction of its pleasures to be adequately conveyed.

IV. BACKGROUND OF THE PERFORMANCES

TRAINING OF THE ACTOR

A Nō actor's training begins in his infancy and may continue until his last tottering appearance on the stage. As a small child he hears from the next room the sounds of his father rehearsing or of pupils being instructed, and he absorbs the words and intonation of Nō almost as easily as those of normal conversation. By the time he is five he makes his debut, delighting the audience with his piping in high monotones of lines whose meaning undoubtedly escapes him. He will have learned by rote every word, every gesture he so awkwardly (but winningly) performs, patiently guided by his father. Only the son of an actor is likely to receive this training from the cradle which, connoisseurs of Nō insist, is indispensable to a truly professional actor. Indeed, the pedigree of an actor of Nō or Kyōgen is so vital a consideration that it is almost unthinkable that an outsider could achieve eminence. Conversely, the actor who can boast the finest pedigree in his school may succeed to the headship even if he himself is an indifferent performer.

Gradually the boy actor moves from token appearances to *kokata* parts which require skill in both recitation and dancing. By the time he is thirteen or fourteen he may assume his first *tsure* part. It sometimes happens today, as often in the past, that a boy who has become the head of his school because of his pedigree rather than his superior talent will take *shite* parts even at ten or twelve. Save in rare instances of genius little more can be expected of so youthful a *shite* than a display of boyish charm.

Some boys, the sons of *waki* actors, are trained in the *waki* roles, resigned from childhood to the fact that no matter how proficient they may become as actors they can never hope to become the star of a play; by tradition, actors of the *shite* and *waki* schools do not cross the lines of their specialities.

At sixteen a promising young actor may be entrusted with his first *shite* role. Usually he begins by performing as a young warrior, particularly in the later Nō plays. Energy and agility (reminiscent of the flying squirrel at the bottom of Zeami's Nine Levels) are considered far easier for an actor to project than the elusive qualities of roles with little movement; the crown of an actor's career, as we have seen, is the performance of the almost motionless roles of old women. The actor gradually progresses up the scale towards roles requiring inner rather than outer display.

The young actor's training is demanding and sometimes painful. Hōshō Kurō kept as mementos of his favorite pupils their practice-books stained with the blood from nosebleeds induced by intense rehearsals. Instruction is mainly oral, though the pupil keeps the text open before him. The teacher sits before a little desk, his pupil facing him at his own desk on which the text rests. The teacher pronounces a line and the pupil, guided more by his teacher's voice than by the notations on the text before him, repeats the line again and again until the teacher is satisfied. The method of instruction in Kyōgen is entirely oral, practice texts not being available. The teacher explains neither the meaning of the words nor the mood they are intended to convey, but insists instead on exact, unquestioning conformity to his own delivery. The pupil parrots the teacher, never attempting to "get inside" the sense of the exceedingly involved poetry. The teacher aids the pupil's recitation by beating time with a small leather baton, but he never suggests that, say, the pupil "give more feeling" to his delivery. When the pupil comes to perform the dances and other movements of the roles, he is shown precisely the number of steps to take at a given moment or the prescribed manner of opening a fan, but not how he is to preserve the flow of movement necessary to a graceful performance. The pupil imitates exactly, avoiding any suspicion of making a fresh attempt to penetrate a role. Only once he has proved that he has mastered the routine techniques will he be initiated into the secret traditions, and only long afterwards will he perhaps interpret the roles slightly differently from his predecessors.

The insistence on imitation and the absence of systematic instruction in performing the texts have resulted in even mature actors at times being ignorant of precisely what they are singing or representing. In extreme cases, as we know from the biographies of distinguished actors, a veteran performer may be unacquainted with the plot of a play in which he has appeared countless times, never having deciphered the language. The Nō actors seem to embody in their voices and gestures the profound beauties of the texts, but their understanding of the parts may be physical rather than mental, and they may lack the intellectual capacity to appreciate why audiences should wish to spend their time and money to attend Nō. Iwakura Tomomi once dismissed with aristocratic disdain all Nō actors except Hōshō Kurō as "monkeys" in the tradition of *sarugaku* ("monkey music"), but even Hōshō Kurō, whose whole life was consecrated to preserving the true traditions of Nō, once expressed amazement that anyone should prefer watching a Nō play to a wrestling match. The lack of intellectual involvement, far from lowering the level of performances, has accounted for the faithful preservation of tradition. The danger today is that young actors, far better educated than their predecessors, will be distracted from a unique concern with Nō into dabbling with other dramatic styles, or may attempt to modernize and rationalize an art which has thus far withstood the assaults of change.

Some changes, however, may become necessary. Sitting in Japanese style on the wooden boards of the stage, surely never comfortable for anyone, has become agonizingly painful for the younger members of the chorus, whose daily lives (unlike those of actors of the past) are spent mainly in rooms with chairs. When at a New Year performance *Okina* is followed by *Takasago*, the chorus and the drum *(taiko)* player must remain in a kneeling position for three hours, a feat of endurance increasingly distasteful to the younger generation. Again, the arbitrary division of the roles into *shite* and *waki*, the latter even following texts of the plays which differ in details from those performed by the *shite*, has been preserved by family traditions for centuries, but ambitious young actors now seem disinclined to become *waki* and play a perpetual second fiddle to the *shite*. Eventually it may be necessary to open all roles to talented actors, and to provide some more comfortable way of sitting for the chorus.

Even more serious than changes dictated by the physical comfort or vanity of the performers are the objections, usually unspoken, against the organization of each school around an *iemoto*, or head. The *iemoto* system, established during the Tokugawa period, was favored by the government, which found it convenient and philosophically desirable to deal with the actors (like other members of the society) in a hierarchical manner, issuing its commands to the head of a school who, like the head of a family, was responsible for the transmission and execution of the order. The system is by no means absolute today, but the head of the school still possesses privileges and obligations that strike the younger generation as being "feudalistic." The head of the Kanze school, for example, is entrusted with the scrolls which explain secret traditions of performing each part. When an actor is qualified to have the secrets imparted to him, the head of the school, with the utmost display of decorum, opens the scroll and reveals only so much of it as is necessary for the particular part. The head of each school normally represents it at cultural festivals sponsored by the government, even if he happens not to be the most distinguished performer of the school, inevitably giving it a bad name among outsiders. The head of the school sometimes also disciplines actors, as a father might discipline a wayward child; two Kyōgen actors who appeared in a Kabuki play were temporarily forbidden to perform in Kyōgen because they had "abandoned their profession." It is hard to imagine an opera director refusing to permit a singer to appear on his stage because the singer had ventured for a few weeks into the domain of musical comedy, but the *iemoto* of Nō and Kyōgen is a father who worries about his children's marriage, drinking habits or lapses from the true path of the art. Needless to say, disciplinary action by the *iemoto*, however benevolently intended, is now often resented.

If the head of a school happens to be its outstanding performer, as for many years Kita Roppeita was not only the finest actor of the Kita school but of the entire world of Nō, the *iemoto* system will not weigh excessively on the actors, who will feel grateful for the prestige the *iemoto* lends to his disciples. Even at its worst, the *iemoto* system has tended to prevent economic hardships among the actors by providing each man with opportunities to perform and a fair share of pupils. The maintenance of the artistic integrity of a school would certainly be infinitely more difficult if no central authority exercised vigilance against departures from orthodoxy and offered the only criticisms which an actor genuinely respected. The five schools—Kanze, Hōshō, Komparu, Kongō and Kita—provide a welcome variety of performance, but the fortunes of the smaller schools are governed by the strength of the *iemoto*'s determination to maintain the traditions. The two largest schools, Kanze and Hōshō, play so dominant a role that the other schools sometimes have difficulty in assembling a competent chorus.

THE SCHOOLS OF NŌ

The five schools have preserved their traditions with a pride commensurate with their long histories. Actors have been known to declare that they never witness Nō presented by another school, either because they fear they may corrupt the purity of their interpretations, or simply because they are totally uninterested in divergent interpretations. The connoisseur of Nō has no trouble in distinguishing among the schools, as a Western music critic will easily identify the mellowness of Central European strings, the clarity of French woodwinds, or the overall brilliance of an American ensemble. To anyone less than an expert, however, *Matsukaze*, regardless of the school, like a Schubert symphony regardless of the nationality of the orchestra performing it, is more likely to leave an impression because of its intrinsic beauty or because of the skill of the performers, rather than by the fidelity it displays to a particular tradition. But the parallel between schools of Nō and European orchestras is far from exact; the variations in the tonal quality of orchestras are apt to be unintentional or even accidental, but the differences among the schools of Nō are so jealously preserved that, the story goes, families will refuse to give their daughters in marriage to men who have studied—even as amateurs—the wrong school of Nō!

The first difference marking the schools is the texts. Textual variants can be found for each play, especially in the prose parts. In extreme cases whole scenes are dissimilar. In presentations of the *shimogakari* (Komparu, Kongō and Kita) schools, *Dōjōji* opens with dialogue accompanying the hanging of the great temple bell, but this scene is omitted from the Kanze and Hōshō presentations. The title of the play may differ according to the school: thus, the work called *Kurozuka* by four of the five schools is called *Adachigahara* by the Kanze school. In some instances, though the title is pronounced identically irrespective of school, the characters used for the sounds differ. *Yuya* is written with characters meaning literally "bear field" by most schools, but the Kita school uses characters meaning "hot water valley."

The repertories also vary from school to school, Kanze boasting the most plays, Komparu the fewest. In 1878 Hōshō Kurō removed thirty plays at a stroke from the repertory of the Hōshō school, some because he considered them inferior, others because their special demands made it impossible for the *iemoto* to guarantee they could always be performed. (*Futari Shizuka*, for example, requires two actors whose build and style of acting will permit them to appear as doubles.) The different schools formerly clung to certain plays as their special possessions, and if another school wished to acquire one of them for its repertory an exchange would be made. This system has now broken down; a work like *Motomezuka*, formerly performed only by the Hōshō and Kita schools, has been borrowed freely for their repertories by the other schools.

Variations in the text are emphasized by special acting traditions called *kogaki* ("small writing"). The *kogaki* employed in the performance of a play is written in small print after the title in the programs, indicating some departure from standard practice. The *kogaki* were probably devised originally so as to prevent spectators from becoming bored by overly familiar representations of the plays; so well were they acquainted with each work that even a slight shift of emphasis could surprise and excite. Sometimes the variation provided by a *kogaki* consists merely of the *shite* wearing a white instead of a red wig for the part of a demon. This seemingly inconsequential difference is elevated to the importance of a major aspect of the performance. An actor deemed insufficiently senior to wear a white wig would be severely criticized. The *kogaki* are learned by the actor only at the appropriate stage of his career and on payment of the regulation fee. Their importance stems from the conviction that altering any element in a play involves a changed conception of the entire performance. For example, *Takasago* is generally performed without any stage prop, but some *kogaki* require a pine tree. In this case, the *shite*, coming to the line, "I shall rake the dust under the tree," must perform the gesture of raking fallen pine needles. The *kogaki* of some schools prescribe a rake rather than a broom for the *shite* in keeping with this change.

Such variations in performance are less important than the stylistic differences among the schools, apparent to the connoisseur. The Komparu school is considered to preserve the old style of performance most faithfully; one authority characterized its singing as "melodic in an old-fashioned way with a placid delivery." In contrast, the Kanze singing has been called "delicately melodic with a nuanced delivery," and the Kita singing "martial in its delivery." The Kongō school is noted for its vigorous, sometimes acrobatic, dancing, in contrast to the extreme restraint of the Hōshō school. The wealth of a school may accentuate its style of performance: the Hōshō school can costume ten *tengu* (demons) for a performance of *Kurama Tengu*, but the Komparu and Kita schools would be hard-pressed to costume more than two or three *tengu*. A school may also follow a particular interpretation of the unspoken implications of a play. In *Yuya*, for example, the mistress of Munemori begs permission to return home, where her aged mother is supposedly dying. Munemori at first refuses, insisting that she accompany him when he visits the cherry blossoms at Kiyomizu, but eventually he relents. She joyfully takes leave, hurrying off to her mother's sickbed. In one school, however, the actor playing the girl is supposed to suggest by almost imperceptible variations in accent that she is less concerned about her mother's health than about rejoining a boyfriend at home. The text does not readily support this interpretation, but its novelty may appeal to spectators looking for something new to admire in a work they know only too well.

Differences of school in Kyōgen are easily apparent even to the casual spectator. Not only do the texts differ markedly, as noted, but the intonation of the lines is totally dissimilar, that of the Izumi school resembling modern Japanese more closely than that of the Ōkura school. Differences in the repertory are also considerable.

THE MASKS

Masks are the lifeblood of a performance of Nō. A great actor may move us even if the mask he wears is inferior, but a beautiful mask can make his performance immortal. Some masks have been registered as national treasures and are displayed in museums, but as the late Kongō Iwao wrote, "The true value of a mask is revealed only when worn by a performer on the stage. There a superior mask can become a part of the actor's body by dint of his superior artistry; it is alive and his blood courses through it. The true beauty of a mask may be sensed at just such moments, and it is just such masks that teach us the spirit of Nō."

It is not easy for an actor to make the audience believe that the mask he wears is part of his flesh. His success is the culmination of efforts begun as a boy of twelve or thirteen. This was the age when, prior to the Meiji Restoration, he would undergo the "coming of age" (*gembuku*) ceremony, and it is still the age when a mask is fitted to the boy's face for the first time, generally the sacred mask of the old man in *Okina*. This is his initiation at once into the world of adults and of Nō. The young man is permitted afterwards to perform with any mask, excepting only those of the middle-aged woman or the old person. At first he is likely to perform roles in which he previously appeared without a mask, like the youthful god in *Makura Jidō*. He is trained to keep the mask steady, avoiding jerky movements or abrupt (and therefore ugly) raising and lowering of the head. By fifteen or so he is ready to put on a young woman's mask, not as a *shite* but as a *tsure*. The *tsure* roles are generally not especially difficult, but it is no small task to wear the mask in a manner evocative of feminine beauty. The apertures in the eyes of the mask are merely holes which permit the actor at best a glimpse of the customers in the balcony. If he wishes to discover where on the stage he stands he has only the nostril-openings in the mask to look through. The young actor has all he can do to keep from bumping into the others onstage even without attempting to suggest by his use of the mask feminine loveliness.

By twenty the actor, having overcome the initial difficulties of wearing a mask, will take the part of a *shite*, appearing as a young woman and wearing a *ko-omote* mask. At the same time he may appear as a young warrior in such plays as *Tsunemasa* or *Kiyotsune*, wearing the *chūjō* mask. Next he moves on to roles requiring the *heita* mask—the powerful, mature warriors of such plays as *Tamura* or *Yashima*. In his thirties he will study female *shite* roles of the fourth category, wearing the *shakumi* mask in *Fujito* or *Sakuragawa*. He may then progress to the roles of gods and demons, wearing the appropriate masks, to the great female *shite* roles of the third category, and finally, when past sixty, to the parts of old women, wearing the *yase-onna* mask in such works as *Sotoba Komachi*.

The progression from one category of role to the next implies increasing difficulty in interpreting the roles but also increasing beauty in the masks used. It might seem more logical for a young man to appear as the beautiful Matsukaze rather than a man in his fifties—probably in Zeami's day a young actor in fact took the part—but it is assumed today that an actor could not evoke the full poetry of the role unless he had spent many years on the stage. He could not, for that matter, employ the mask to the full effect, adumbrating the shades of emotion by causing shadows or glints to fall on his mask. He would also be unworthy of wearing a mask of the highest dignity (*kurai*). Not only do the masks differ in dignity according to their category (whether for a young general, a young woman or a devil), but also according to the quality of a particular mask within the same category. Sometimes this is a matter of artistic excellence: many masks, particularly of the Muromachi period, rank as masterpieces of carving, and to perform with such a mask is not only an honor but a responsibility. The story is told of Hōshō Kurō's visit to Kyoto with his disciple Matsumoto Nagashi. The young man was to appear in *Tenko*, and Kurō asked the head of the Kongō school if he might borrow a *koujijō* mask for the occasion. The mask offered him was so magnificent that Kurō refused it, saying that young Matsumoto was not yet sufficiently accomplished to merit such an honor.

Even among masks of approximately equal artistic value a difference in "dignity" may arise because one is almost imperceptibly older, severer in expression or more dreamlike than another. The different schools are known for their preferences in these matters: the Komparu actors prefer *ko-omote* masks of a childlike innocence, the Kongō actors a slightly more sensual face, and at the other extreme, we find the almost voluptuous expression on the *ko-omote* masks used by the Kanze school. When Hōshō Kurō appeared twice within a short time in *Sumidagawa*, an admirer remarked that one interpretation had seemed quite astringent, the other almost youthful. Kurō, pleased to find such acuteness of appreciation, took out the two *shakumi* masks he had worn, one aged, the other youthful. The different interpretations of the role had grown from a week or more studying each mask. The slightly different "dignity" had inspired different performances. That is why an actor desires several masks of the same category. As Kongō Iwao put it, if an actor has only one *magojirō* he can express only one level of dignity *(kurai)* in the role, but if he has five *magojirō* masks he can perform five different interpretations of *Matsukaze*. The *kurai* of the mask also determines the costumes used, and it is said that unless the musicians and the members of the chorus know the *kurai* of the *shite's* mask they cannot perform.

The actor's greatest problem in the use of the mask is giving it expression. The female masks especially are virtually blanks as far as the expression goes. Scholars have argued over whether this "intermediate expression" was intended to represent feminine beauty at its most evocative, or to be a straightforward depiction of a lovely face in a moment of repose, or a symbolic representation of the essential nature of a woman's character; but the researches of Gotō Hajime indicate that the neutral expression of the female masks much antedates the age of Zeami, when the ideal of *yūgen* might have inspired symbolic delineation of the features. No doubt the "intermediate expression" was adopted for masks in order that the actor might suggest without changing his mask the joy or grief of the character. Certainly the female masks are so used today. A lowering of the mask *(kumorasu)* casts shadows suggestive of grief, a raising of the mask *(terasu)* lightens it, giving an expression of happiness. Needless to say, the use of the mask is far more subtle than a mere raising and lowering. In *Nonomiya*, for example, at the lines "Whom should I pine for now? The voices of pine-crickets trill *rin, rin . . .*," the actor, who must not resort to any obvious gesture of listening, lowers his gaze to the chirping insects, then gently moves his head laterally in the gesture known as "seeing a voice." The effective use of any mask is difficult, but in comparison to the delicacy required in *Matsukaze* or *Nonomiya*, the warrior plays are relatively uncomplicated in expression, the masks less demanding. The ascending order of the roles is also an ascending order of difficulty in using the masks, culminating in the great plays *Sotoba Komachi* and *Sekidera Komachi*, in which the actor must convince us by the way he uses his mask that beneath the skin of the aged crone there is still a beautiful woman.

Some roles, especially in the *genzaimono*, are performed without mask. In these cases it is hardly an exaggeration to say that the actor's face becomes a mask, that there is hardly more individuality in the face of a great actor performing without mask as Benkei in *Ataka* than in a warrior mask. The Kyōgen actor appearing as Sambasō in *Okina* who repeats again and again the meaningless, incantatory syllables *yo hon ho*, by the end of the performance becomes as impersonal an embodiment of good fortune as the masked old man Okina himself. In the parts performed without mask the *kurai* comes from the innate personality of the actor. The effect is the opposite of the masked roles where the actor endeavors to infuse a carved piece of wood with expression; here the actor must drain the expression from his face into his voice and body. In either case the effect achieved is a stylized and evocative beauty remote from the representational effects of actors on other stages.

Though the roles without masks may be as demanding as those performed with masks, the mask is the symbol of the Nō actor, and the moment when he puts on a mask before a performance marks the transition from his daily existence to the special realm of his art. Before the actor places the mask on his face he stares at it intently, holding it at the two small holes of the ears, the only part of the polished surface which should be touched. The actor's face is padded with wadded cotton wrapped in soft paper so that the mask will fit snugly and securely. The mask is attached to his head by ribbons passed through the ear-holes. The color of these ribbons varies with the mask: white for *okina*, red for *kokushiki*, purple for a woman's mask worn by a *shite*, dark blue for a woman's mask worn by a *tsure*, and so on. The ribbons from the left and right ears must be attached with equal tautness if the actor is to see at all. Originally, it seems, the ribbons holding the mask to the face were concealed by the wider bands attached to the wig, but today the wig is fastened below, leaving the mask ribbons exposed.

The masks are made of *hinoki* (Japanese cypress), a wood easily worked yet durable. The bark side of the wood is fashioned into the inside of the mask; in this way any resin which might seep to the surface will not harm the mask. Ideally, the *hinoki* wood for the masks should come from trees felled in the Valley of Kiso, floated down the Kiso River to Tokyo, and kept there for five or six years in mingled fresh and sea water before being cut into the blocks used by the mask-carver. Wood of this quality is scarce today, but the best available is always used, for the Nō mask is a work of art.

Most masks are about eight and a half inches in length, the width varying somewhat according to the variety. They are too small to cover the actor's entire face, but generally leave a disillusioning sallow or reddish fringe of jowls around the lovely contours of the painted wood. The smallness of the mask may have originated in an aesthetic ideal of a small head on a large body, though Japanese more often have large heads on small bodies. Audiences in the past, seated at a distance from the badly lighted stage, were undoubtedly far less aware of the actor's jowls than we are today from our seats a few feet from a stage brightly lit with fluorescent lamps.

Aesthetic ideals apparently also gave rise to the extraordinarily high foreheads of the masks of young women. The proportions of the forehead are accentuated by the shaved eyebrows and the false eyebrows painted almost at the hairline. The Muromachi fashion for a high forehead and shaved eyebrows, curiously coincidental with the similar fashion in Europe of the time, is perpetuated in the masks, along with the severe part of the hair in the middle. New masks have been devised and the prevailing tastes of later ages have found unconscious expression, but for the most part the masks, like the Nō itself, adhere to models created in the fifteenth century.

The earlier masks, as we know from examples preserved in temples and shrines, showed far greater variety. Some are startlingly realistic, the faces of men and women one might encounter today. No doubt these masks reflect the plebeian origins of Nō. Unlike *gigaku* or *bugaku*, Nō in the thirteenth and fourteenth centuries was a popular entertainment, performed at inconspicuous temples in the hills—anywhere an audience could be attracted—as well as at the great monasteries. The plays surely lacked the exalted manner of Nō in its full glory, and the countrified expressions on the masks suggest little of *yūgen*. Indeed, the masks may originally not have been intended to afford greater beauty than the commonplace face of the actors; they may have been intended instead to make the actors resemble the characters they portrayed, whether a girl, a middle-aged woman, a general or a demon. The old masks usually have a definite expression. Those for young women have smiling mouths and eyes crinkled with merriment, indications that the plays themselves were not the melancholy vehicles now associated with the name Nō. The features, it should be noted, are distinctly Japanese, unlike the *gigaku* and *bugaku* masks, which were faithful copies of prototypes from the Asian continent. The techniques of carving the early Nō masks may have been borrowed from those of the *bugaku* masks—*bugaku* was widely performed when the Nō masks were being created in the thirteenth and fourteenth centuries—but the faces are entirely dissimilar. Even the devils represent peculiarly Japanese conceptions rather than the leonine *bugaku* features. The old masks are true products of the lively theatricals performed before Nō acquired its unique dignity as a court entertainment and the categories of masks were formalized.

The masks today may roughly be divided among the three roles mentioned by Zeami—the old person, the woman, and the warrior—plus the demons. Within each category numerous variations occur. The young woman, for example, may be a girl between sixteen and twenty, as in *Yuya* (*ko-omote* mask), or between twenty and twenty-five, as in *Eguchi* (*magojirō* mask); she may be possessed by a demon like Rokujō in the first part of *Aoi no Ue* (*deigan* mask), or a divine being like the angel in *Hagoromo* (*zō no onna* mask); she may be brooding like Kiyohime in the first part of *Dōjōji* (*Ōmi onna* mask) or griefstricken like the mother in *Sumidagawa* (*shakumi* mask). Each school maintains different traditions and sometimes different names for the masks. The individual actor, moreover, is at liberty to experiment somewhat in the choice of mask for a role in the interests of a slightly altered emphasis. A few masks are used for a single role only, like that for Yorimasa, a man aged but still warlike; for Shunkan, emaciated and deeply embittered; or for Yoroboshi, a blind young man of haggard appearance. (The masks for the roles of blind persons have long, downcast slits for the eyes instead of the usual tiny apertures, paradoxically affording the best visibility to the actors!)

The most distinctive masks are those of the demons. *Beshimi* masks have mouths tightly shut in a frown, and lines in the face denoting strength cluster around the forehead and cheeks. The effect, however, is more comic than frightening, and the mask is used for *tengu*, the rather genial demons. By contrast, the small *beshimi* (*ko-beshimi*) masks, much closer to normal human features, are marked with evil unrelieved by exaggeration. Most terrifying are the different varieties of *hannya*, a horrible grinning mask with horns, the incarnation of feminine possessiveness. The name *hannya*, ironically, means "wisdom" (from the Sanskrit *prajna*), but here it probably comes from the maker, Hannyabō.

The names of sixteen celebrated mask-makers have been preserved from Muromachi times, some mentioned in Zeami's writings. Prized masks today are almost all attributed to these men, but clearly many attributions are legendary, and others refer to a workshop rather than to an individual. The profession of mask-maker was recognized only in the Tokugawa era. Until then, we may gather, masks were often made by priests or general artisans rather than by special artists. Many superlative masks are undoubtedly old copies of even older works. Such makers as Kuoji, Tokuwaka, Himi, Echi and Shakuzuru are solemnly credited with many extant masks, but probably no more can be said about these revered names than that they represent characteristic styles. Certainly the degree of sophistication in the carving of many masterpieces does not accord with the early dates—some in the Kamakura period—assigned to these men. Kongō Magojirō (1538–64), whose name was taken for the female mask typifying the Kongō school, is one of the earliest mask-makers we can date.

Three *ko-omote* masks attributed to the legendary Ishikawa Tatsuemon acquired special fame as prized possessions of Hideyoshi. The masks, known as the "snow," "moon," and "flower" *ko-omote*, were left by Hideyoshi to the head of the Komparu school, the Shogun Ieyasu, and the head of the Kongō school respectively. The "moon" mask was lost in a fire, the "flower" mask has been disfigured by clumsy restoration, but the "snow" mask, now owned by the Kongō school in Kyoto, is a particularly lovely *ko-omote*, considered by some experts to be the most perfect mask of all.

Kyōgen masks, far fewer than those for Nō, fall into four main categories: Shinto and Buddhist divinities, spirits, human beings, and animals. The deities include the god of good fortune, Bishamon (a Buddhist protective divinity), Lightning, and Dragons; the spirits include Buaku and Usobuki, two typical Kyōgen figures; the human beings include Grandpa, the Ugly Woman (Oto), and the Nun; the animals consist of the fox, the badger, the monkey, the ox, the dog and birds. Buaku, a comic villain, wears a grotesque version of the Nō mask *beshimi:* the eyes droop, the cheeks are extraordinarily broad, the teeth protrude and bite the lower lip. The *usobuki* mask has pursed and twisted lips and great goggling eyes; it is used to represent the spirit of a mosquito (in *Kazumō*) or of a cicada (in *Semi*) or of a mushroom (in *Kusabira*) or, occasionally, a pathetic-looking robber (in *Uri-nusubito*). Normally the Kyōgen actor does not resort to using a mask in order to indicate that he is playing the part of a woman, but for comically ugly women the *oto* mask is used. Oto has a bulging forehead and cheeks, a nose squashed almost flat, and a comically twisted mouth. The Nun's mask is sometimes an older version of *oto*, sometimes amusingly lachrymose in expression.

The Kyōgen masks are far from realistic, but just as the Nō masks seem to symbolize the essential traits of a role, the Kyōgen masks exaggerate and distort them. Ugliness, timidity and even ferocity become funny thanks to the masks.

The masks, whether Nō or Kyōgen, are never worn without a wig or head covering. In Kyōgen a towel or a simple hood *(zukin)* will serve as covering, but the Nō masks require a wig in one of three lengths: *katsura, tare* or *kashira*. *Katsura*, not generally used for male roles, are black wigs parted in the middle, covering the ears and pulled back. *Tare* are longer, falling to the shoulders; they are always worn with a *kammuri* or head ornament, which may be a hat, a crown, or another kind of headgear. Some *tare* are white rather than black, and are used for aged gods or warriors. The third variety of wig, *kashira*, hangs down in back as far as the hems of the robe or even to the floor, in front to the actor's chest. The *kashira* exists in black, white and red: black is for a wide variety of male roles, white for aged persons, red for demons. The wigs are fastened to the head by a broad, decorated cloth band, the ends of which hang down behind. Some wig bands are exquisite examples of weaving and embroidery. The colors used with a particular wig are determined by the role. An expert, if informed of the mask, wig, wig band and headgear used for the *shite's* part, should be able to name the play.

THE COSTUMES

The brilliance of the Nō costumes relieves the performances from any impression of excessive severity that might be created by the astringent bareness of the stage, the harsh cries of the musicians, and the formal gestures of the dancers. In Zeami's and Zenchiku's day the costumes were probably far less elaborate than today, and possibly even in bad taste by modern standards; we can infer this from the description of a costume worn in *Bashō* ("The Plantain Tree"), which was to be suitably ripped here and there to suggest the easily torn leaves of the plantain tree.

The oldest surviving Nō robes, dating from the reign of the Shogun Yoshimasa in the fifteenth century, may have been woven for the Shogun himself, as their sober but elegant taste indicates. One owned by the Kanze family, a jacket *(happi)* of dark green material woven with gold thread in designs of paired dragonflies, is a lovely but unassertive robe. We can imagine Yoshimasa removing his jacket and throwing it to the actors in admiration, rather in the manner of a Spaniard throwing some article of clothing into a bull ring by way of homage to a toreador. The presentation of robes by way of reward goes back at least as far as Zeami's day. By the seventeenth century it came to be a gesture of affluence on the part of daimyos towards the actors they maintained. During the Tokugawa period the robes attained a degree of elegance and luxury unparalleled in theatrical costumes elsewhere. Some were woven or embroidered in silks with breathtakingly bold patterns of plantain leaves, enormous butterflies, wisteria sprays, or ships riding the waves; others were covered with finely figured designs in geometric or floral patterns; still others had patches of contrasting, brilliant colors and designs. The robes were woven in heavy brocades or translucent gossamer silks, and the blend of the colors, whether on the surface of the robes, between one layer and the layer underneath, or between the surface and the lining, was in flawless, though sometimes daring, taste.

The Nō costumes are without exception splendid, whether the actor appears as a princess or a fishergirl, a general or a priest, but the colors and designs are modified according to the roles. The costumes for the female roles are divided between those with and without "color" *(iro)*. By "color" was meant red, associated with young women and worn with the *ko-omote, waka-onna* or *magojirō* masks in such plays as *Matsukaze* or *Yuya*. Roles performed with the *shakumi* or *fukai* masks (like the mother in *Sumidagawa* or the jealous wife in *Kinuta*) are costumed in robes without "color." Color is not, of course, used in costuming old women, though there are a few exceptions: the *shite* in *Sotoba Komachi*, though a woman of a hundred years, wears a touch of red in her sash or cloak to suggest that something of the beautiful woman lingers about her. If red is used for the outer robe the color is usually echoed in the wig band, the sash and even in the fan. These hardly visible touches of color help to create a unified impression. On occasion, as when a young god is portrayed, a brilliant red sash, contrasting with the white or pastel color of his robe, produces an effect of youthful vigor.

The colors of the under-kimonos, visible at the neckline, are also important indications of the "dignity" of the role. The colors may be single, double or triple, each variation signifying a difference in character. White, red, light blue, dark blue, ultramarine, light green, russet, yellow-brown and brown are the chief colors used. White is the most dignified, green and brown the least dignified. Red stands for youth, high spirits, good fortune; light blue for a quiet temperament; dark blue or ultramarine is used for strong roles; light green is generally reserved for menials, and the browns for old people. The use of white under-kimonos in a play of the third category marks the role as of the highest "dignity"; more commonly, the neckline will show one white and one red under-kimono. In *Shōjō* two red under-kimonos are worn by the auspicious red-maned demon, and as acted by the Kongō school the demon is further graced by red *tabi* on his feet. Because red is somewhat less dignified than white it is the invariable color of youthful female *tsure*, of some male *tsure*, and of all *kokata*. The *waki* usually wears a light blue under-kimono. A combination of one white and one light blue under-kimono adds dignity to a role.

Each actor before appearing onstage chooses the costume for the part according to the emphasis he desires to give the role, the mask to be worn, and the holdings of his school. Strong traditions dictate the costumes to be worn for certain roles: the snake-lady in *Dōjōji* always wears a robe with a lozenge pattern suggesting a snakeskin. Nevertheless, the actor enjoys some leeway in his shading of most roles. When a play is revived after long absence from the Nō stage the costuming is particularly important. At the revival of the rarely-performed *Ochiba* ("Fallen Leaves") by the present Kongō Iwao, the entrance of the *shite*, wearing a *chōken* (long-sleeved jacket) of a mingled green and brown, evocative of fallen autumn leaves, created an unforgettable impression. This superb garment was a modern reweaving of a *chōken* originally presented the school by the Shogun Yoshimasa.

The articles of clothing worn, including the many varieties of headgear, reveal the function and dignity of the persons. No less than twenty-eight costumes have been distinguished for the male roles performed without mask. Twenty or so distinct types of attire for female *shite* and *tsure* exist, and there are comparable numbers for all other parts, including the Kyōgen. The Nō robes, originally derived from the costumes of the court and military nobility (and the priesthood), were later modified so noticeably that they came to constitute a distinct variety of dress seen only on the stage. A typical robe worn by men and women alike is the *mizugoromo*, a kind of cloak. The *mizugoromo* occurs in white, black, gray, violet and most pastel shades, depending on the role. Most often it is unpatterned and woven of raw silk into a thin gauzy material. When worn in a male role a sash is tied over the *mizugoromo*, but in female roles it is held together by a silken cord. Each detail of the costuming is governed by usage, down to the type of fan carried and whether or not it can be tucked into the sash of the *mizugoromo*. Details of the costumes are discussed elsewhere in connection with the accompanying photographs.

The mask and costume used by an actor in a particular role reveal almost as much about his interpretation of the part as his singing and dancing. The mask and wig give him the face of his choice, the voluminous robes, all but blotting out the outlines of his own figure, give him the shape prescribed by aesthetic ideals, and the most glorious colors ever used to adorn the human form surround him in beauty. The eyes of the spectators are dazzled by the sight of the *shite*, but the purpose of the mask and costume is not so much to attract attention and praise as it is to allow the spectator, undistracted by ugliness, to take these exquisite passages into a realm of absolute beauty.

V. MUSIC AND DANCE IN THE PLAYS

MUSIC

For the hundreds of thousands of amateurs who study the singing of the texts Nō is primarily a vocal art and the actors are above all singers. Amateurs who devote themselves to the *shimai*, the climactic dances in the plays, may disagree about the importance of song, but they recognize equally that music is essential to their dances. The scholar of literature, it is true, may read the Nō plays as if they were verse dramas, not thinking of the music he is missing, but a performance without music would be unthinkable. The stranger to Nō may nevertheless find that the music, though hypnotically impressive, lacks the variety common to most other music for the stage, a variety stemming both from alternations of mood and tempo and from the distinctive styles of different composers. The music in Nō lacks obvious contrasts of mood, and it would be almost impossible to identify the composers. Its importance also seems to be thrown in doubt by the tolerance of the poor voices of many actors. The great Hōshō Kurō went so far as to deplore the tendency, prevalent in his day, for actors to rely on the beauty of their voices to win acclaim; this, he insisted, was contrary to the emphasis on interpretation characteristic of Nō. Even at their most lyric, the songs of the *shite* rarely attain an independent existence as melody; only in the sections sung by the chorus is it easy to detect the melodic element, which sounds—to the non-musician at least—rather like the Gregorian chants. The man witnessing Nō for the first time may find the music to be the most elusive aspect.

The difficulty of Nō music comes both from its complexity and its dissimilarity to familiar Western music. The texts used by the actors are marked with dots, curved and angular lines, and letters of the Japanese syllabary, each indicating the manner in which a particular syllable is to be delivered. A rise or fall in the voice, a shift from declamation to recitative or to full voice, can be prescribed, but these markings (dating back to the sixteenth century) give only the relative pitch and length of the notes, not absolute values. A mark indicates that a sound is held twice as long as the preceding one or that it is higher in pitch, but not the note that might be played on a piano. Neither is the tempo of the successive notes stated except vaguely, in recommendations that a passage be "quietly" rendered and the like. The annotations serve as a guide or reminder to students of Nō, but they must turn to their teachers for instruction. Even then they will discover that ultimately the singing of a role, like the dance, depends on the actor's understanding of its "dignity" (*kurai*), and his ability to suggest by means of vocal techniques unknown in the West the inner natures of the characters he portrays.

The simplest parts of the play are those in prose, sometimes a third or more of the whole. These passages, which bear almost no musical notation, are declaimed in a style marked by regular cadences; in particular, the second note after each pause in a sustained utterance is delivered at a noticeably higher pitch. In some schools the pattern of declamation depends on whether the actor is representing a man, a woman or an old person; in others no distinction is made. Despite the mournful prolongation of the words the prose parts are in general intelligible to the audience. They are delivered without musical background.

It is rather misleading to speak of the "accompaniment" for the sung parts. The "name saying" (*nanori*) at the start of the play is sometimes "accompanied" by a flute, but the flute neither blends with nor opposes the singer's vocal line; its music proceeds virtually independently, decorating or heightening the passage, but not commenting on it. Even the drums "accompanying" the singer may not play at his tempo. Indeed, one feature of all Nō music is its irregularity; the range required of the singer's voice being extremely limited and the musical patterns established by long tradition, slight differences in tempo or accent assume great importance, and the mood evoked by the musician's hand against a drum or by his inarticulate cries evokes the poetry better than would an accompaniment which merely echoed or reinforced the vocal line.

Two styles of singing Nō are distinguished, *yowagin* (weak) and *tsuyogin* (strong). Different styles of singing apparently existed even in Zeami's day, but the present distinction of "weak" and "strong" dates only from the late seventeenth century. Previously, *yowagin* was used exclusively. *Yowagin* can be rendered with reasonable accuracy in Western musical notation, but *tsuyogin*, closer to declamation, hardly goes beyond two distinguishable tones. In contrast to the rich melodic patterns of some passages delivered in *yowagin*, in *tsuyogin* "accent, dynamic stress, tone color, and a special vocal technique are more important than melodic movement itself."* *Yowagin* predominates in most plays, especially in scenes of heightened emotional content, but *tsuyogin* occurs in auspicious or festive plays like *Takasago*.

The vocal music includes sections like the *issei* or *kuri* in free rhythms, and others in fixed rhythms, such as the entrance song (*shidai*) of the *waki*, the travel song (*michiyuki*), and passages of dialogue between the *shite* and chorus. There are three basic rhythmic structures: the first, a majestic, regular beat called *ō-nori*, links each beat to a single syllable; the second, the fast *chū-nori*, links one beat to two syllables; and the third, the *hira-nori*, distributes the twelve syllables of a normal line of Nō poetry (consisting of two verses of seven and five syllables respectively) among eight beats. Of these three rhythmic patterns the last, the *hira-nori*, is by far the most common. Its pattern tends to fall into two sections: the first fits a seven-syllable verse into four and one-half beats, the second fits a five-syllable verse into three and one-half beats. This is done by giving the first, fourth and seventh syllables double the duration of the others. The final beat is usually a pause, plus the beginning of the next beat. The counting of the beat therefore begins not at "one" but at "eight," taking over from the end of the previous section. Many variations exist, but adequate discussion involves technicalities beyond a layman's competence. The rhythms of Nō in any case are flexible, not metronomic; indeed, musicians avoid metronomic regularity as carefully as some Western musicians cultivate it.

Nō gives pleasure to many solely as music, but to the actors the music is the natural outgrowth of the sounds and meanings of the words and of the overall "dignity" of the play. The melodies, whether in such purely instrumental sections as the opening flute solos or in the sustained passages of choral singing, are rarely unique to a particular play, though the combinations form peculiarly appropriate patterns. There is never any improvisation in the performance—every sound, to the last cry from a drummer and the part of his drum he strikes, is noted in the score—but flexibility in the rhythm and tempo enables the actor to impart to his singing an individual interpretation of the roles.

The statements by the great actors on their preferred way of singing the roles afford some clues to their interpretations. Kanze Sakon (1895–1939) wrote about the *waki* part in *Takasago:* "The *waki*, being a minister of state, should sing forcefully and clearly, without faltering. His entrance song, this being a Nō play of the first category, should be delivered with greater forthrightness

*From the excellent article "Japanese *Noh* Music" by Tatsuo Minagawa in *Journal of the American Musicological Society,* Vol. X, No. 3, (1957).

than a normal entrance song. In general, the actor should attempt in singing the *waki* role to preserve a smoothly flowing line." Sakon went on to describe the entrance song *(shin no issei)* of the *shite* and *tsure* in the same play: "The *shite* enters, accompanied by the *tsure*, and sings the entrance song. This passage, as the first song by the *shite*, determines the *kurai* of the piece and is therefore most important. It should be sung loudly and firmly with a relaxed but solemn feeling. The actor must not impart to it sticky, heavy or listless feelings."

The manner in which the music may affect the actor's performance is indicated by remarks of Umewaka Manzaburō (1868–1946) concerning the "woman" plays: "By the time the *waki* has made his entrance the "dignity" of the play should already have been established. Of course, a clear distinction must be made between the music accompanying the *waki*'s entrance song and that found in a god play or a warrior play. This distinction is all the more essential for the entrance of the *shite*; the musicians must exercise sufficient care so that there will be plasticity in the accompaniment. Any lack of understanding on the part of the musicians will make it extremely difficult for the actor even to step out on the *hashigakari*, let alone to travel along the *hashigakari* to the stage. If the musicians let the tempo get out of hand, the *shite* will be forced to race down the *hashigakari*, for he has no choice but to move his feet ahead in step with the *ya ha* of the accompaniment."

Specific recommendations on the manner of singing Nō are apt to be unintelligible to the layman, and even the devoted student of Nō can hardly be guided much by the constant injunctions to maintain grace and dignity. The present head of the Kanze school, Kanze Motomasa, suggests the great emphasis given today to the psychological analysis of a play like *Kagekiyo* : "Even if I were to attempt to treat each problem involved, I could not hope to explain everything. The student has no choice but to follow his teacher's instructions. He should practice the opening passage again and again until satisfied." Motomasa added, "If a student has been able to analyze exhaustively the character of Kagekiyo, he has already succeeded eighty percent with the opening song. Of course, the musical line here is one of unusual difficulty even within the entire repertory, and any belief that analysis of the character alone suffices would lead to serious mistakes. But if the student combines with an adequate command of the melodic line a complete understanding of the role, then practices beyond all normal demands, he will probably pass as a fair singer of *Kagekiyo*."

The delivery of the Nō actor cannot be judged by the standards of Western singing, for no attempt is made to delight by the beauty of sound alone. The different voices—tenor, baritone or bass—are not distinguished intentionally, and certainly there is no exploitation of the extremes of the voice, whether the ringing high notes of the tenor or the growling depths of the basso. A hoarse, quavering or thin voice is not considered a flaw in an older actor, and a younger actor will also be forgiven an inadequate voice if he manages somehow to convey the inner meaning of the texts. The Hōshō school insists that singers produce a "lower voice" together with their normal tones, a complexity in vocal production intended, no doubt, to parallel the complexities of meaning in the text, which easily results in a strong vibrato. The voice, regardless of school, is produced in the back of the throat, altering the quality of the vowels and contributing to the obscurity of the words. A novice taking his first lesson from a teacher of the Komparu school is likely to be informed that it is a feature of the singing of this school to open the mouth wide but never show the teeth; what this does to the diction can be imagined. The peculiarities of the delivery certainly interfere with intelligibility, but the spectators (who either know the texts by heart or consult printed versions) expect the actors to interpret the words rather than enunciate them. The voice itself becomes a special kind of musical instrument, no less than the drums and flute.

Of the instruments used in the Nō ensemble the flute is closest to its Western equivalent. It is some fifteen inches long, made of bamboo, and has seven apertures in addition to the mouth-hole. The flute is the only instrument capable of sustaining a melody, but the thin, sometimes shrill notes are apt to produce an effect of disembodied sound rather than the sweetness associated with the Western flute; the two are as dissimilar as the mad women in Nō and the unhappy heroine of *Lucia di Lammermoor*, who goes mad to a flute accompaniment.

The *kotsuzumi* and *ōtsuzumi* are unlike any Western instrument. Each is shaped like a diabolo, the *kotsuzumi* being covered with coltskin, the *ōtsuzumi* with ox or horsehide. The drums, made of lacquered cherry wood, are kept in tune by six hempen cords fasted to holes in the metal rims at the two ends. The *kotsuzumi* is about eight and a half inches long, the *ōtsuzumi* nine and a half inches; but it is less the difference in size than the difference in the skins drawn over the drum-frames that makes the two drums sound so dissimilar. The *ōtsuzumi* produces a loud and resonant crack, the *kotsuzumi* a more delicate thump. The *kotsuzumi* is grasped by the cords with the fingers and palm of the left hand and held on the right shoulder, where the drummer strikes it with the fingers of his right hand. The quality of the sound depends on the tension of the cords and the place on the skin struck, whether the center or the edges. The *ōtsuzumi* is grasped in the left hand by the cords and placed on the left knee, where the drummer strikes it with the fingers of his right hand. The index, middle finger and palm of the hand are protected by leather coverings against the smart from the taut skin. Unlike the *kotsuzumi*, the *ōtsuzumi* cannot be tuned in performance; this means that the only differences in sound possible are loud and soft, but the expert can recognize whether or not a new drumskin has been used for each performance, as tradition prescribes (but as economic realities rarely permit).

The *taiko*, a large drum, is used in perhaps a third of the plays. It is beaten, like a Western drum, with sticks held in both hands. The *taiko* rests on a low stand placed on the stage, and the drummer, less fortunate than the *kotsuzumi* or *ōtsuzumi* player who sits on a folding stool, must kneel on the stage, sometimes striking the drum from high above his shoulder, sometimes bending to cut off reverberations. The *taiko* is about eight and a half inches in diameter, but the only place struck is a round patch of deerskin about two inches wide pasted at the center.

The sounds of the instruments are accompanied by cries from the players. In general, a player utters a cry (*kakegoe*) before the half-beat. The variety of the cry and the strength of his beat give character to the sound. There are four basic varieties of cries: *ya*, delivered before the first and fifth beats, indicating that it divides the eight beats of a measure in two; *ha*, delivered before the second, third, sixth and seventh (and sometimes the eighth) beats; *iya* and *yoi*, delivered with odd-numbered beats, to demarcate the rhythmic patterns or serve as signals to points of tension.

The music for Kyōgen is far simpler. Most lines are delivered to a rhythmical, though not specifically musical, intonation. The standard opening line of a Kyōgen, "I am a person who lives in this vicinity," is delivered by actors of the Ōkura school as:

       ko*re* wa/ ko*no* atari ni/ *su*mai/ ita*su* mono de/ *gozaru*.

This passage is in prose, but as the contemporary Kyōgen actor Shigeyama Sennojō explains, a rhythmical quality is imparted by giving each group of syllables, whether three or six, about the same length of time and a single accent, without ever slurring the pronunciation of unaccented syllables. Most important to the effect is the ringing Kyōgen voice, which Sennojō's great-grandfather Sengorō Masatora (1810–1886) once compared in vigor and clarity to the sensation of slicing vertically through a piece of green bamboo.

Occasional songs, called *kouta*, are interpolated in the plays. These popular songs of the Muromachi period are far lighter both in content and delivery than the music for Nō; they are, moreover, always identified as songs by the characters and not utterances which are sung. Usually, too, the *kouta* are not accompanied, but in some plays, especially those of a festive nature, drums accompany the dance of a god. In other plays Nō is parodied by having the foolish hero make his entrance to the conventional accompaniment of a flute and drums only to intone such unpoetical lines as, "I am glad to be returning home and I am eager to see my wife and children again." But musical accompaniments of whatever variety are exceptions: the Kyōgen plays are prose, spoken dramas with only occasional outbursts of song.

DANCE

Dance is no less close to the heart of Nō than music. By "dance," however, one should not imagine anything resembling even the stateliest of Western ballets. Some movements called "dance" in Nō seem hardly more than a solemn circling of the stage; others are so slow and so devoid of choreographic ornamentation that it is hard to tell when the dance begins or ends. With the exception of a handful of special dances, like the *rambyōshi* ("wild rhythm") of *Dōjōji*, the dances consist of familiar elements, repeated from play to play, on the surface little related to the actions or the characters. Instruction in performing the *shimai*, regularly published in the magazines directed at students of Nō, is likely to consist of a few diagrams depicting simple triangular or semi-circular patterns of movement and statements such as: "Stand when the chorus sings *the lightning flashing in the trees*; stamp the left foot at the syllable *re* at the end of the phrase *hi ka to koso mire*; at the words *truly the world is like a lightning flash glittering on the morning dew* take four steps forward, beginning with the left foot," and so on. The exact moment to open the fan or to sing a phrase, taking over from the chorus, is clearly stated, but if the dance were no more complex than these injunctions imply, it could not rank as an important part of Nō.

Our experience is quite otherwise. The dances in Nō dominate remembrances of the plays to such a degree that some critics have insisted that the plays themselves are little more than preparations or justifications for the dances. These dances never startle by their pyrotechnics; they are so rarely athletic that, like the singing, they are best performed by aged actors even in the roles of young women or warriors in their prime. An unearthly beauty pervades the dances. Oswald Sickert, writing in 1916 his impressions of the final dance in *Hagoromo*, declared, "The divine lady returned on her steps at great length and fully six times after I thought I could not bear it another moment. She went on for twenty minutes, perhaps, or an hour or a night; I lost count of time; but I shall not recover from the longing she left when at last she floated backwards and under the fatal uplifted curtain."

The movements of the dance are unassertive but they express and epitomize the texts, not by crude miming (though in a few realistic plays the actor's gestures may suggest actions described by the chorus), but by evoking the ultimate meaning, the "dignity" of the work. Kita Roppeita's performance as the angel in *Hagoromo*, even when he was a man in his sixties, enchanted audiences by an atmosphere of remarkable charm. Even at eighty his performance as the *shite*, a white heron, in *Sagi* was filled with a haunting, other-worldly beauty, though he appeared without a mask. By tradition this role is danced only by a boy under twelve or a man over sixty, someone untouched by worldly passions, and as Roppeita danced he communicated a magic power surely partaking of *yūgen*, a quality that could exist only in Nō.

The higher the "dignity" of a play, the fewer and simpler tne movements of the dances; unable to distract by mere virtuosity, the actor must transmute each gesture into symbolic utterance. Some roles, it is true, require great agility. The Kongō school in particular maintains a tradition of acrobatic display in a few plays. But though people still reminisce admiringly about the late Kongō Iwao turning somersaults as the demon in *Tsuchigumo*, even when in his fifties, the Kongō school itself prizes this skill less than the ability to execute with authority the unassertive movements of a *Matsukaze*. The audiences too attend Nō not for brilliance of footwork but for absolute assurance in every gesture of the head, arms, body and legs, an inevitability that expresses the nature of a role better than the most literal display.

We are often told about the glories of the actors of former days, which are contrasted unfavorably with contemporary performances. Normally it is impossible to prove or disprove these assertions, but the film of *Aoi no Ue* made in 1936 by Sakurama Kintarō (1889–1957) reveals an almost unbelievably accomplished performer whose every motion glows with controlled fire. In his later years Kintarō once advised amateurs how they should go about learning the *shimai*: "You should stand erect, your head perfectly straight, pulling your chin back as far as possible. If you pull back your chin your whole body—not only the line of your neck—will naturally be straight. The shoulders should be relaxed, but the arms kept at the sides and held in a gentle arc so that the elbows will not sag. This is worth noticing; most people, when told to stand erect, at once throw back their shoulders and their body freezes. You should let your strength flow into your abdomen without making any conscious effort to do so. As long as you maintain a steady posture your strength will naturally flow there . . . The small of the back, like the chin, should be pulled back somewhat, but you must avoid protruding the buttocks. The exact posture to be held can only be demonstrated on the stage.

"The first thing the actor must remember while onstage is to walk on his heels. Ordinarily one begins a step with the toes, but in Nō the actor puts his strength into his heels and walks from the heels. If he puts his strength into his heels his toes will naturally curve upwards somewhat. If he were deliberately to attempt to curve the toes it would look unnatural, but if he concentrates on his heels the toes seem to curve upwards of themselves. It is ugly if the actor permits his knees to bend excessively when walking.

"Movements of the eyes are also important. There is nothing less attractive than an actor with unsteady eyes. It sometimes happens that a single glance reveals the emotions of a character."

Dance in Nō has been defined as any action made by the actors on the stage, for not one motion is unpremeditated. In a narrower sense, dance can be defined as movements by the actor to the accompaniment of a flute at a time that the chorus is not singing. Dancelike movements executed while the chorus is singing and which may or may not be related to the words of the song are known as *kata*, or forms. These highly stylized gestures are best considered in terms of photographs. They provide much of the element of *monomane* ("imitation of things") in a performance, though far removed from literal representation. The *kata* provide intermittent clues to the texts, but the dances of Nō, usually abstract patterns, are almost synonymous with the art itself.

The varieties within each of the five categories of Nō dramas are distinguished as much by the dances as by the subject matter; indeed, the dances and subject matter are inseparable and affect the entire structure of each play. Two main divisions are made: *mai* and *hataraki*. *Mai* are recognizable as dance by their length, solemn atmosphere and complexity of movements, but *hataraki* may be so simple as hardly to seem dances. Often the *hataraki* consist of vigorous, even wild, steps, and are used especially for fierce gods or demons. The *hataraki*, unlike the *mai*, are generally not performed to the same rhythm as the accompanying flute. The *mai* contain no elements of representation, but the *hataraki* may embody *kata* which refer to the texts.

Seven varieties of dance can be found in plays of the first category, the god plays, alone: *kamimai* ("god dances"), *hataraki*, *gaku* (dances derived from *bugaku*), *shinnojonomai* (especially slow and stately dances), *chūnomai* (dances performed by female deities), plus *kagura* and *shishimai* ("lion dance") used in one play each. A play with a *kamimai*, for example, contains such features as: (1) two scenes, the first consisting of the *jo* and *ha* sections of the play, the second of the *kyū*; (2) a dance occurring in the second scene; (3) the *shite* in the first scene appears as an old man of lowly occupation, normally accompanied by another man who does not wear a mask; (4) the *shite* in the second scene appears as a youthful god and performs a vigorous dance to express his appreciation of the worshipers' sincerity, a token of his desire for the protection of the imperial family and the nation; (5) the *waki* as a rule is a courtier, accompanied by two to four attendants.

Obviously the nature of the dance grows out of the plot, which in turn must be made to fit smoothly into the pattern of expression provided by the dance. If the story tells of an aged god rather than a youthful one, the dance performed in the second scene must be a *shinnojonomai*. In this case the *waki* will be a Shinto priest rather than a courtier. Again, if there are two dancers a *hataraki* will be used; the *shite* of the first part, whether a man or a woman, will wear a mask of less exalted "dignity" than for a *kaminomai* or *shinnojonomai* role; and the costume will be plebeian. A mixture of the elements proper to different dances does not occur.

The typical dance in the warrior plays is called *kakeri*, a relatively short and simple dance usually performed by the *shite* as he enacts his confession of the sins of violence which have brought him torture.

Plays of the third category are almost all about women, though in two the *shite* is the poet and great lover Narihira. The dances are slow and elegant; more than half are *jonomai*, a dance of the slowest tempo. In these plays the *shite* of the first scene is a village woman of humble birth, but normally the same mask is retained for the second scene where she appears as a noblewoman. The *waki* is an itinerant priest. In some works a *taiko* is added to the accompaniment. This creates a somewhat livelier atmosphere, and the "dignity" is therefore lower than that of plays without the *taiko*. Another group of third category plays is of a more realistic nature and in one scene, like *Yuya*. Here the dance is a *chūnomai* of a faster tempo.

The fourth category contains the greatest variety of plays and dances, including those like *Hanjo* with a graceful *chūnomai* for the *shite*, a woman; or like *Semimaru* with an agitated *kakeri*; or like *Sotoba Komachi* with a brief *iroe*, a gliding about the stage rather than a dance; or like *Kanawa* with a fierce *inori* ("prayer") dance by which a demon is subdued; or like *Shunkan* with no dance at all. These plays rely less on the beauty of the dance (which may be the core of a work like *Matsukaze* or *Hagoromo*) than on what it contributes to the dramatic tension. It might be said of certain plays of the first or third categories especially that they are excuses for dances, but in plays of this category if the action does not require a dance, none is performed.

Plays of the fifth category, belonging to the fastest section of the program, almost all have *hataraki* rather than *mai*, regardless of the plot. A typical work concludes with the furious prancing of a demon, but in the special case of *Funa Benkei*, the *shite* of the first part is given a *chūnomai*, performed in the semblance of Shizuka, the beautiful sweetheart of Yoshitsune, as well as a *hataraki* in the second part, performed as the fierce ghost of Tomomori.

In addition to the *mai* and *hataraki* mentioned above, which figure in almost every Nō play, a few dances are performed in one work only, including the three different dances of *Okina* and the *rambyōshi* in *Dōjōji*.

The effortless lines described by a master actor's body as he moves in a dance are the despair of the amateur. Though the movements are simple in themselves, they approach a perfection that can be sensed though not measured in terms of the height of a leap, the number of entrechats, or the other obvious exhibitions of virtuosity in Western ballet. The depth of communication—the ability of the actor to express with his whole body the torment, serene joy or bittersweet longing felt by a character—is the only touchstone of his powers. Every passage in the text is given overtones by the actor's movements, though none may directly represent the words. Criticism of the dances by experts in Nō sometimes suggests to the amateur the emperor's new clothes, a beauty more in the eye of the beholder than in the performance, but repeated experiences in this theatre breed a virtuoso audience no less than virtuoso actors. The Nō actors, with the barest economy of means, achieve in song and dance a grandeur of expression fully intelligible only to spectators who have made comparable efforts to understand this endlessly rewarding art.

VI. THE NŌ STAGE AND ITS PROPERTIES

THE STAGE

The interior of a Nō theatre is unlike any other in the world. It is dominated by the large, gleaming stage projecting into the auditorium, a stage which by its size and majesty seems to assert that even without actors it would have sufficient reason to exist. Its ornate curved roof confirms this impression of independence: the stage, as we have seen, was formerly a separate building, and at the very beginning of its history may have served as the scene of ritual observances before the gods. Today, when the theatre building housing the Nō stage may be fashionably modern, and the audience attired mainly in business suits and Paris-inspired dresses, the stage still imposes its authority, hushing the voices of those entering its presence, even before the performance begins. The absence of a curtain, the unvarying lighting before and during a performance, the great pine painted on the back wall, all suggest less a Western stage—shabby and bare until it takes on life from a play—than a church, itself an architectural masterpiece but ready for the drama of the mass.

Each event that takes place in a performance emphasizes the presence of the stage. In a Western theatre, whether an ornate opera house or an intimate theatre-in-the-round, the stage itself is no more than the platform on which the actors perform. It may be chalk-marked to show the actors where to stand, or grimy with the residue of a thousand nights, or pockmarked with holes. Nothing in the world is so forlorn as a Broadway theatre after a performance, the abandoned set lit by a single, naked lamp. The Nō stage, by contrast, is a superbly finished object of art whose surface is polished rather than scuffed by the actors, their feet shod in white cloth *tabi*. The boards are immaculate. A famous anecdote tells of an actor who was complimented by an expert in Japanese fencing for having maintained an *en garde* position throughout a performance—except for one fleeting moment of uncertainty. "Yes," answered the actor, "that was when I noticed a speck of dust on the stage."

The importance of the stage to the plays is underlined by the precise nomenclature for the different areas and the equally precise functions that have been assigned to each. The *hashigakari*, an extension of the stage, affords superb possibilities for entrances and exits, whether the uncertain steps of the blind Yoroboshi, guided by an inner light, or the precipitous departure of one Kyōgen actor in pursuit of another. Some scenes take place entirely on the *hashigakari*, the actors disposed at the first second and third pines to form a pleasing composition. The railing of the *hashigakari* may also serve a function in the play, as when a demon vaults from it onto the stage. Even the entrance of the musicians at the start of a play is given a solemn dignity by their passage along the *hashigakari* that no entrance from the wings of a conventional Western theatre could approximate.

Once on the stage from the *hashigakari*, the *waki* and the *shite* will each go to his appointed place, and though they move away from time to time, they will presently return. It is not merely that the actors are so strongly bound by traditions that they cannot make innovations; the stage no more permits the *shite* to stand in the *waki*'s place than the rituals of a church would permit the officiating priests to alter their stations in the interests of more powerful dramatic effects. The actor's appearance on the Nō stage presupposes that he will obey its demands.

The actor acknowledges the importance of the stage by his pounding on it during climactic moments of his dances. Unlike the ballet dancer who attempts to create an illusion of weightlessness, the Nō actor insists that he tread the stage. If he leaps in the violent movements of a dance, he deliberately lands with a reverberating thud. Even the ghosts in Nō proclaim their reality by their footfalls.

The stage imposes its aesthetics. The plays, with few exceptions, can be acted without props, but even when props are used, they are never permitted to clutter the clean expanse of the Nō stage or to usurp the audience's attention. The prop—whether a boat, a tree, a hut or a carriage— is hardly more than an outline of the object represented. The boat in *Funa Benkei* is so small that only the boatman, Yoshitsune and Benkei can board it; the other soldiers sit on the stage outside the white frame of the boat in an attitude of being aboard. Of course it would be possible to build a more commodious boat, but the larger the prop the less easily it could be brought on by the stage assistants and removed when no longer needed; moreover, it would break the beautiful lines of the stage.

The present form of the Nō stage dates from the mid-Tokugawa period, when Nō achieved what may have been its final evolution. The earliest stages consisted of pieces of level ground, perhaps beaten earth like the rings for *sumō* wrestlers. Even today the torchlight Nō performances at the Kasuga Shrine in Nara take place on a stage consisting merely of boards over the bare ground. Originally—as at the Kasuga Shrine today—there was no *hashigakari*. The actors made their way to the stage from the dressing room, a curtained-off enclosure some distance away, entering the stage from the rear-center. The pines now planted along the *hashigakari* may be a memento of the trees passed by the actors in former days as they walked through the precincts of a shrine to the stage; similarly, the curtain that shields the mirror room from the *hashigakari* may be the descendant of the curtains around the original makeshift dressing room.

The bridge to the stage gradually developed into a formal architectural feature. At the time of the performances given in 1464 under the patronage of the Shogun Yoshimasa a passageway similar to the *hashigakari* extended from the dressing room to the stage-rear, meeting it perpendicularly. A curtain hid the backstage area beyond the *hashigakari*. Seats were arranged in a large circle around the stage: the area directly in front of the stage was reserved for the gods, and the best seats (adjacent to the gods') were occupied by the shogun (to the left) and his consort (to the right). Less favored guests sat at the opposite side of the circle, near the *hashigakari*. The presence of an audience on all sides suggests a style of performance dissimilar to that of Nō today, but the actors probably concerned themselves with pleasing the spectators directly before them— the gods and the shogun.

In the early Muromachi period the *dengaku* stage had two *hashigakari*, one on either side, presumably in imitation of the practice of *bugaku* dancers of entering from both left and right. Not long after the 1464 performances the Nō actors began to experiment with attaching the *hashigakari* to a side of the stage rather than to the rear. At first the *hashigakari* extended to the stage at stage-left, by the flute pillar, but presently it was switched to stage-right, by the *shite* pillar, perhaps because the side closer to the shogun's seat was considered more important. When stages came to be built within the compound of a daimyo's palace, less spacious than a Shinto shrine, the angle made by the *hashigakari* and the stage, at first almost forty-five degrees, steadily decreased. Today the horizontal boards of the *atoza* merge almost imperceptibly with those of the *hashigakari*.

By good fortune two magnificent old Nō stages have been preserved. The first, at the Itsukushima Shrine on the Inland Sea, was built in 1568 as an offering to the shrine by Mōri Motonari (1497–1551), a powerful warlord who found time amidst his more than two hundred military campaigns to become expert in poetry and the arts. The stage at Itsukushima is built so close to the sea that high tide flows between the stage and the spectators, creating the illusion that the realm of the plays is separated from our own not only by time and space but by the sea. The stage stands about three and one-half feet above the water. Its pointed roof thatched with *hinoki* bark and its unpainted pillars (unlike the satiny gleam of the pillars at other Nō stages) have a weather-beaten look that makes the contrast with the brilliant costumes all the more striking. The *hashigakari* from the dressing room meets the stage at rather a steep angle and its boards, instead of joining those of the *atoza*, cut across to those of the stage proper. The *hashigakari*, thatch-roofed like the stage, stands on stone posts, the better to resist the erosion of the sea water.

The stage at the Nishi Honganji Temple in Kyoto was originally constructed for Toyotomi Hideyoshi about 1595 and moved to its present site in 1626. It is still in use, together with a smaller practice stage which is slightly older. Seated in the temple hall surrounded by magnificent gold screens along the walls, it is easy for the spectator as he watches the plays today to imagine himself a daimyo. Beneath the eye-level of those seated in splendor within the hall stand the ground-lings on the gravel of the area around the stage. The elaborately carved horizontal beams under the stage roof are a further reminder of the grandeur of Hideyoshi's palace and of his great devo-tion to Nō. The *hashigakari* joins the stage, a separate building, at an angle conspicuously less acute than that at Itsukushima. The Nishi Honganji Temple stage may have been the first pro-vided with large jars underneath for resonance—seven under the stage proper, two under the *atoza*, and three under the *hashigakari*. These jars are suspended by copper wires over pits in the ground to provide the maximum effect.

The conservatism of the Nō theatre accounts for its retaining the roof for the stage, the gravel bed around it, the steps leading down—all meaningless today in terms of function. Even the number and shape of the metal rings used to hold up the curtain at the end of the *hashigakari* have been carefully prescribed. Yet there have also been many changes, some unconscious, others re-flecting almost imperceptible shifts in taste. A modern Nō theatre is equipped with the latest com-forts, including an up-to-date restaurant that has largely replaced the lacquered lunch-boxes of the past, and the pine of the backdrop may be distinctly of the twentieth century, an angular tree that startles us by its unconventionality.

Some innovations have been adopted only after a long struggle. When it was first proposed that electric lights be installed in the Nō theatres, the conservative Hōshō Kurō and Umewaka Minoru were flatly opposed. Kita Roppeita, a younger *iemoto*, was willing to experiment, but at first allowed only one small light bulb and insisted that the audience be warned in advance that electricity would be used. Umewaka Minoru's son (who took his father's name) later recalled, "My father, a man of the old school, was curiously obstinate in some respects. In 1905 Mr. Iwasaki Yanosuke had complained that the stage was too dark when lit by candles only, and pro-posed that electric lights be installed, but my father was absolutely opposed. At the time, the theatre had two candles on either side of the steps at stage front, two before the *waki*'s seat, three on the *hashigakari*, and two thick candles in square glass boxes at the *kōken*'s seat and by the flute pillar. Mr. Iwasaki kept urging that these candles be replaced by electricity, and finally won the day when he pointed out that the glass boxes we were already using were no less foreign than electric lights."

The stage itself has changed little in recent years, but if future members of the chorus are unable to sit for prolonged periods on the wooden boards it may become necessary for stools or chairs to be provided, undoubtedly entailing some modification of the entire stage.

THE PROPS

Many plays are performed without props, but when used they add much to the visual pleasure of Nō. Yuya's journey to the blossoming cherry trees at Kiyomizu is given special brilliance by the carriage in which she travels. This prop is no more than a rudimentary evocation of the wheels and hood of a real carriage, but when Yuya stands inside to the accompaniment of music of suddenly heightened intensity, we feel poignantly the contrast between the loveliness of the blossoms and the sad thoughts of Yuya, who fears her mother may be dying. The prop lends a charm and pathos to the scene all out of proportion to the simple means employed.

Props are usually brought in along the *hashigakari* by the stage assistants before the play begins. In some plays, however, the prop is used only in the second part. It is particularly effective if the *shite* is first revealed to us when the wrappings of the prop, which represents a hut or a palace, are removed by the stage assistants. In *Kagekiyo* the wrappings drop away to disclose the old warrior in his hut, blind and despondent. If the character made his entrance along the *hashigakari* in the normal manner, the overpowering impression of withdrawal from the world would be much diluted. The hut in which Kagekiyo sits is barely large enough to hold a seated man. Once the wrappings are removed all that is left is four bamboo poles holding up a tiny thatched roof. The actor's appearance at that moment should be a clear indication of his interpretation of the entire role, whether he will emphasize the pathetic fate of the defeated warrior or the dignity of a man proud even in adversity. When at last Kagekiyo, having rejected his daughter, emerges from the hut, the prop makes this moment intensely moving. Of course the adept of Nō could easily visualize the pathos of the moment, even without the prop, but the flimsy little structure is more affecting than the hut that might be conjured up by the imagination.

Some elaborate props are used, like the great bell in *Dōjōji* into which the snake princess leaps, the platform ornamented with huge peonies used for the demons' dance in *Shakkyō*, or the chrysanthemum garden evoked by the prop in *Makura Jidō*. A few plays require props representing mountains or grave mounds from which the *shite* makes his appearance; usually these props are wrapped round with cloth and covered at the top with leaves to suggest the mountain vegetation. Pines, cherry trees and plum trees are represented by a standing branch held up by a square or circular frame. In *Izutsu* a frame with a spray of pampas grass represents the well-curb, and in *Hachinoki* the prop represents dwarf trees in their pots.

In addition to the stage props the actors often carry swords, halberds, sickles, Shinto wands, flower baskets, and a large variety of other objects intended to heighten their appearance in particular roles. Unlike the stage props which are dismantled after a performance, the accessories are solid, if often smaller-than-life, objects. The actor sometimes carries an accessory in his hand from his entrance, but in many plays he goes to the *atoza* and accepts the sword or cloak he will use from a stage assistant, returning it in the same manner when no longer needed. The stage assistants also produce the lacquered cylindrical cask which serves as a seat for the *shite* during moments of repose. This cask is commonly used in Kyōgen too, where it may represent a great variety of objects.

By far the most important of the accessories is the fan. Hardly a role in Nō does not require a fan. The signal for a dance by the *shite* is his lifting of the fan he keeps at his waist and opening it. The fan is not only indispensable to the dances of the *shite* but may be used, especially in Kyōgen, to represent other objects—a flask of saké, a saké cup, or a deadly weapon.

The importance of the fan in Nō reflects its peculiar role in Japanese life. A fan formed a part of formal attire in the past, and even today it is customary at New Year for ordinary citizens to carry a fan when making their first calls. As early as the eleventh century a fan was carried by military men when in attendance at court, and there are numerous accounts of court ladies, priests and others giving and receiving fans as presents on special occasions. The pictures painted on the fans include some counted among the masterpieces of Japanese art.

Three types of fans are used in Nō. The first, called *uchiwa*, is round and does not fold. A Chinese invention, it is carried only by Chinese personages in the Nō plays. (A variant, the enormous feather *uchiwa*, is carried by *tengu*, the feathered demons, as part of their outlandish getup.) The fan most commonly used in Nō is the *chūkei*, a folding fan. The folding fan was a Japanese invention—it was in fact a principal article of export to China during the Muromachi period—and its association with Japanese dance goes back at least to the twelfth century, when the *shirabyōshi* dancers beat time for their dances with a folding fan. *Chūkei* means something like "spread out from the middle," referring to the flaring out of the upper part of the fan. The *chūkei* used in Nō has fifteen ribs, either black or white (actually, the natural yellowish color of the bamboo). Black-ribbed fans are used for all female roles and for many male roles; white-ribbed fans for the roles of old men and priests. Fans with white ribs have monochrome paintings on white paper, but the fans with black ribs are decorated with brilliant colored scenes, the subjects determined largely by the category of the play. Fans used in plays of the first category in which the *shite* is a god are likely to bear a painting of phoenixes sporting among paulownia leaves and flowers. If the *shite*'s role is that of an old man, the painting on his fan may be a *sumie* representation of the Seven Sages of the Bamboo Grove. The design of fans used in plays of the second category, the warrior plays, depends on whether the *shite* is victorious or vanquished. The victorious warrior's fan has a design of the rising sun amidst pine branches; the defeated warrior's shows the sun rising amidst the waves, reminiscent of the Heike clan, which perished at sea. Plays of the third category, the woman plays, often use fans with brightly colored pictures of carriages filled with flowers or of court ladies carrying sprays of blossom in a "flower tournament." However, if the *shite*'s role is of an old woman the design may be of autumnal flowers or camellias. The obsessed women depicted in plays of the fourth category carry fans with a double design of profusely blossoming clematis and pine branches, no doubt to suggest the warring emotions in the *shite*'s mind. Fans carried by the demons in plays of the fifth category usually depict a peony in full blossom against a vermilion ground. The *waki* if a priest carries a fan with a design of the moon among the clouds, an allusion to the peripatetic life of the traveling monk. Certain roles require special designs, and variations exist from school to school. The *chūkei* used in Kyōgen are less rigidly prescribed in subject, but tend to be parodies of the beauties depicted on the Nō fans, showing for example a huge turnip on a golden ground.

Another variety of fan, called *shizumeori*, is more like the fan used in daily life. It is carried by actors in some roles performed without mask, and also when dancing the *shimai*, the climactic dances of the plays, in "concert versions," wearing an ordinary formal kimono instead of the costume for the role. Members of the chorus also carry these fans, placing them on the stage before them until about to recite, then raising them as in ceremonial utterance. The *shizumeori* fans bear different designs for each of the five schools of Nō: a pattern of swirling water for Kanze, five-fold clouds for Hōshō, five "dumplings" for Komparu, nine "dumplings" for Kongō, and three-fold clouds for Kita. The Kyōgen *shizumeori* also indicate the school: a design of young pines in the mist for Ōkura and usually a design of snowflakes in a circle for Izumi.

The handling of the fan is an essential part of the dancer's art, and each motion is as carefully prescribed as the steps of the feet. The fan accentuates the motions of the arm and lends grace to gestures, particularly the characteristic sweeping movements found in the Nō dances. Of all the stage props and accessories it is the most pervasive, and so indispensable that Nō has been spoken of as a kind of drama performed with fans.

Compared to theatres elsewhere in the world and even to other varieties of Japanese theatre, Nō and Kyōgen depend very little on props and accessories. The stage offers nothing to distract the audience, certainly nothing in the nature of the facile realism of representational theatres. Even such accessories as swords or spears are not intended to convince by any realistic glint of metal. The stage props help create the illusion of a particular place or atmosphere; the accessories help to distinguish the persons, rather as a wheel, tower or handkerchief may distinguish a medieval saint and tell us the nature of her suffering or triumph. But however effective the props may be in their functions, they are dispensable; representation in Nō depends far less on the props and accessories and even the costumes than on the basic elements, the stage and the masks.

PLATES

1 and 2. *Takasago* Kongō School
A priest on his way to the capital visits the Bay of Takasago, known for its great pine tree. He finds an old couple sweeping fallen pine needles, and eventually learns that this man and woman are the spirits of the pines at Takasago and Sumiyoshi. He continues his journey to Sumiyoshi, where the god of the place appears and, after telling of his age-old protection of the Imperial House, dances and promises to bring joy to the people. (A god play)

(1) The old woman, the spirit of the Takasago Pine, enters carrying a broom, followed by the old man, the spirit of the Sumiyoshi Pine.

(2) The old man and woman, now on the stage, remain seated as the chorus sings of the glories of the Takasago Pine. The priest and his companions also listen.

◁ 5. *Genji Kuyō*   Kongō School
Some priests visiting the Ishiyama Temple are asked by a woman to say a memorial service for Prince Genji. She says that her failure to include such a service in her novel has kept her from gaining salvation. When asked if she is not Lady Murasaki, the author of *The Tale of Genji*, she disappears without answering. In the second part she confesses she is Murasaki. The priest promises to pray for Genji. (The photograph shows Murasaki's gesture of gratitude.) (A woman play)

6. *Yuya*   Kita School
Yuya, the favorite of the nobleman Munemori, learns that her mother is seriously ill. She asks permission to return home to the country, but Munemori insists that she accompany him and see the cherry blossoms. Later she composes a poem expressing her feelings so poignantly that Munemori permits her to go. Here she reads the letter in which her mother describes her illness. (A woman play)

◁ 7. *Izutsu*   Kanze School
A priest visits the Ariwara Temple where, many years earlier, the famous lover Narihira had lived with the daughter of Ki no Aritsune. As he prays, a young woman appears. She speaks of the past, especially of how she and Narihira as children had compared heights while standing by a well-curb (*izutsu*). She disappears, only to return, this time wearing the hat and cloak Narihira gave her. Here she pushes aside the bush of flowering *susuki* to peer into the depths of the well. She sees Narihira's reflection, not her own. (A woman play)

8. *Sotoba Komachi*   Hōshō School
Some priests on their way to the capital encounter an old woman. Gradually she reveals she is Komachi, and tells of her former beauty, contrasting it with her present wretchedness. As she speaks, the spirit of the man she treated cruelly possesses her, and she speaks in his voice. At the end, as she describes his death, she hopes she may yet gain salvation. Here, dressed in her lover's cap and cloak, she dances as she recalls in his voice the ninety-nine fruitless visits he paid her before he died. (A fourth-category play)

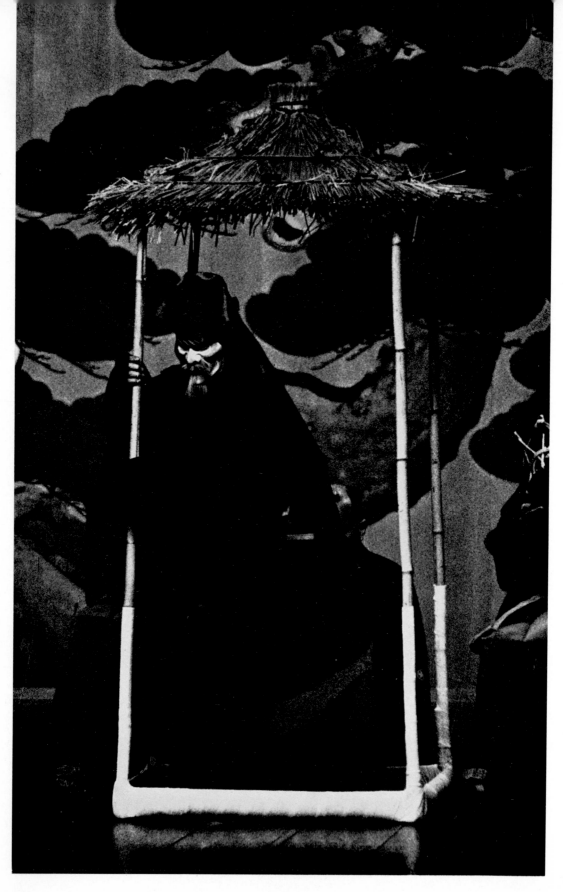

9. Kagekiyo   Kanze School

Kagekiyo, a defeated Heike warrior, is living in exile. His daughter visits him, but he is too proud to let her see him in his present state. He turns her away, denying he is Kagekiyo, but a villager informs the daughter that the man she has met is her father. She returns, and this time he admits his identity. He describes his last battle, standing in his hut. (A fourth-category play)

10. Semimaru   Kanze School

Semimaru, the fourth son of the Emperor Daigo, is blind. His father gives orders that he is to be abandoned on Ōsaka Mountain. His sister Sakagami discovers him in his lonely hut, but after a moment of recognition the two must part. Here, Semimaru, still wearing his princely robes, is guided by a courtier to his hut on the mountain. (A fourth-category play)

12. *Kagyū*　　　Izumi School
Tarōkaja is ordered by his master to go into the ▷
woods and find a snail. The master uses *kagyū*,
a difficult word for "snail," describing it in such
terms that Tarōkaja, bumping into a *yamabushi*
(mountain ascetic), supposes he is a "snail." The
yamabushi is much amused by the mistake. (Kyōgen)

11. *Tsuchigumo*　　　Kongō School
The warrior Raikō is afflicted by a mysterious illness. A priest
informs him that the illness is caused by a great spider (*tsuchigumo*).
Raikō sees through the priest's disguise and recognizes that he is the
spider. They fight, and the wounded spider flees. In the second part
a retainer of Raikō tracks the spider to its lair and kills it. Here, the
spider attempts to enmesh the retainer in its web. (A demon play)

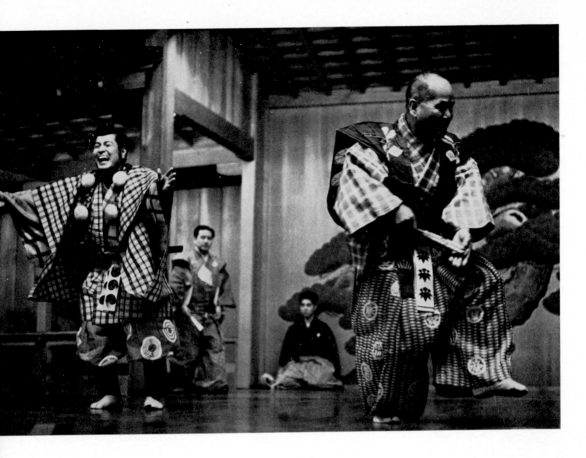

13. *Kirokuda* ("Six Loads of Lumber")   Ōkura School
A certain gentleman sends his servant Tarōkaja with six ox-loads
of lumber and a cask of saké for his uncle. It is bitter cold, and
Tarōkaja, stopping at an inn, drinks some of the saké to warm
himself. As he gets drunk he explains to the proprietor how he
plans to catch in his arms a quail, to eat with the liquor. (Kyōgen)

14. *Votive Performance at the Itsukushima Shrine*
At high tide the waters of the Inland Sea flow around the
stage, separating it from the audience. To the right the
Great Torii is faintly visible in the water.

15. *Nō at Chūsonji*
At the annual festival of the temple, Nō plays are presented
in the open air, amidst the majestic trees.

16. *Okina* by Nikkō. Umewaka Collection. $6\frac{1}{4}'' \times 5\frac{3}{4}''$.
This *okina* mask, used only for Sambasō in the play *Okina*, is of the oldest type. It is characterized by the *kiriago* ("split jaw"), meaning that the mask is in two pieces, tied together with string. The black variety is less aristocratic in features than the other two kinds of *okina* mask, and is well suited to the comic Sambasō role.

17. *Koujijō* by Kouji. Kongō Collection. $7\frac{7}{8}'' \times 6\frac{1}{4}''$.

The great dignity of this mask makes it appropriate for the roles of old men who prove to be earthly manifestations of gods, like the *shite* in the first part of *Takasago*.

18. *Ōakujō* by Shakuzuru. Kanze Collection. $9'' \times 7\frac{3}{4}''$.

This mask is used for powerful, frightening old men; its large size accounts for its name, meaning "large *akujō*."

19. *Yoroboshi* by Yamato. Kongō Collection. 8⅛″ × 5½″.

This mask of a blind boy is worn by the *shite* in *Yoroboshi*. The boy, falsely accused and disowned by his family, goes blind through grief and must beg for a living. The mask powerfully suggests his tragic fate.

20. *Rōjo* by Himi. Umewaka Collection. 8″ × 5¾″.

This is the mask of an old woman who once had been beautiful. It is especially suited for the role of Komachi, and is worn in *Sekidera Komachi* and *Sotoba Komachi*. The face reveals the character's age, but there are no wrinkles, a lingering reminder of her former loveliness.

95

21. *Ko-omote* by Tatsuemon. Kongō Collection. 8¼″ × 5⅜″.
The cheeks of this mask are full, the forehead wide, and the face
suffused with youthful beauty. This particular mask is known as the
yuki ("snow") *ko-omote*; it was one of three *ko-omote* masks by
Tatsuemon prized by Toyotomi Hideyoshi.

LIST OF NŌ PLAYS CURRENTLY PERFORMED

Unless otherwise stated, plays are performed by all schools.

OKINA (翁) (first play)
　　Author unknown
ADACHIGAHARA (安達原) (demon play)
　　Author unknown
　　Referred to as *Kurozuka* by schools other than
　　Kanze
AIZOMEGAWA (藍染川) (miscellaneous play)
　　Author unknown
　　Performed by Kanze and Komparu schools only
AKOGI (阿漕) (miscellaneous play)
　　Attributed to Zeami, but Zeami probably reworked
　　text of an earlier play
AMA (海士) (demon play)
　　Author unknown, but work antedates Zeami
AOI NO UE (葵上) (miscellaneous play)
　　Adapted by Zeami from an Ōmi *sarugaku* play
ARASHIYAMA (嵐山) (god play)
　　by Komparu Zempō
ARIDŌSHI (蟻通) (miscellaneous play)
　　by Zeami
ASHIKARI (芦刈) (miscellaneous play)
　　Adapted by Zeami
ASUKAGAWA (飛鳥川) (miscellaneous play)
　　Attributed to Zeami
　　Performed by Kongō and Kita schools only
ATAGO KŪYA (愛宕空也) (demon play)
　　by Kanze Kojirō Nobumitsu
　　Performed by Kita school only
ATAKA (安宅) (miscellaneous play)
　　by Kanze Kojirō Nobumitsu
ATSUMORI (敦盛) (warrior play)
　　by Zeami
AWAJI (淡路) (god play)
　　by Kannami
　　Performed by Kanze, Komparu and Kita schools
AYA NO TSUZUMI (綾鼓) (miscellaneous play)
　　by Zeami
　　Performed by Hōshō, Kongō and Kita schools
BASHŌ (芭蕉) (woman play)
　　by Komparu Zenchiku
CHIKUBU SHIMA (竹生島) (god play)
　　Author unknown
CHŌBUKU SOGA (調伏曾我) (miscellaneous or demon
　　play)

　　by Miyamasu
　　Performed by Hōshō, Kongō and Kita schools
CHŌRYŌ (張良) (demon play)
　　by Kanze Kojirō Nobumitsu
DAIBUTSU KUYŌ (大仏供養) (miscellaneous play)
　　Author unknown
DAIE (大会) (demon play)
　　Author unknown
DAIROKUTEN (第六天) (demon play)
　　Author unknown
　　Performed by Kanze school only
DAMPŪ (壇風) (miscellaneous or demon play)
　　Author unknown, but attributed to Zeami
　　Performed by Hōshō, Kongō and Kita schools
DŌJŌJI (道成寺) (miscellaneous play)
　　by Kanze Kojirō Nobumitsu
DŌMYŌJI (道明寺) (god play)
　　Attributed to Zeami
　　Performed by Kanze, Kongō and Kita schools
EBIRA (箙) (warrior play)
　　Attributed to Zeami
EBOSHI ORI (烏帽子折) (miscellaneous play)
　　by Miyamasu
　　Performed by all schools except Komparu
EGUCHI (江口) (woman play)
　　by Kannami
EMA (絵馬) (god play)
　　Author unknown
　　Performed by all schools except Komparu
ENOSHIMA (江島) (god play)
　　by Kanze Yajirō Nagatoshi
　　Performed by Kanze school only
FUE NO MAKI (笛之巻) (miscellaneous play)
　　Author unknown
　　Performed by Kanze school only
FUJI (藤) (woman play)
　　by Hiyoshi Saami (?)
　　Performed by Kanze, Hōshō and Kongō schools
FUJISAN (富士山) (god play)
　　Probably by Zeami
　　Performed by Kongō and Komparu schools
FUJI TAIKO (富士太鼓) (miscellaneous play)
　　Attributed to Zeami
FUJITO (藤戸) (miscellaneous play)·

Author unknown, but generally attributed to Zeami
FUNABASHI (船橋) (miscellaneous play)
　　Adapted by Zeami from a *dengaku* Nō
FUNA BENKEI (船弁慶) (demon play)
　　by Kanze Kojirō Nobumitsu
FUTARI SHIZUKA (二人静) (woman play)
　　Author unknown
　　Performed by all schools except Hōshō
GEMBUKU SOGA (元服曾我) (warrior or miscellaneous play)
　　by Miyamasu
　　Performed by Kita school only
GENDAYŪ (源太夫) (god play)
　　Probably by Kiami
　　Performed by Komparu and Kita schools
GENJŌ (玄象) (demon play)
　　Author unknown
GENJI KUYŌ (源氏供養) (woman play)
　　Attributed to Zeami
GENZAI NUE (現在鵺) (miscellaneous or demon play)
　　Author unknown
　　Performed by Komparu and Kita schools
GENZAI SHICHIMEN (現在七面) (miscellaneous play)
　　Author unknown
　　Performed by Kanze and Kongō schools
GENZAI TADANORI (現在忠度) (warrior or miscellaneous play)
　　Author unknown
　　Performed by Kongō school only
GIŌ (祇王) (woman play)
　　Attributed to Zeami
　　Performed by Hōshō, Kongō and Kita schools
HACHINOKI (鉢木) (miscellaneous play)
　　Author unknown
HAGOROMO (羽衣) (woman play)
　　Author unknown
HAJITOMI (半蔀) (woman play)
　　by Naitō Tōzaemon
HAKURAKUTEN (白楽天) (god play)
　　Author unknown, but usually attributed to Zeami
　　Performed by all schools except Hōshō
HANAGATAMI (花筐) (miscellaneous play)
　　by Zeami
HANJO (班女) (miscellaneous play)
　　by Zeami
HASHI BENKEI (橋弁慶) (miscellaneous play)
　　Author unknown
HATSUYUKI (初雪) (woman play)
　　by Komparu Zempō
　　Performed by Komparu school only
HIBARIYAMA (雲雀山) (miscellaneous play)
　　Attributed to Zeami
HIGAKI (桧垣) (woman play)
　　by Zeami
　　Performed by all schools except Komparu
HIMURO (氷室) (god play)
　　by Miyamasu
HIUN (飛雲) (demon play)
　　Author unknown
　　Performed by all schools except Komparu
HŌJŌGAWA (放生川) (god play)
　　by Zeami
HŌKAZŌ (放下僧) (miscellaneous play)
　　Author unknown, but probably by Miyamasu
HŌSO (彭祖) (miscellaneous play)

Performed by Kongō school only
　　Author unknown
HOTOKENOHARA (仏原) (woman play)
　　Attributed to Zeami
　　Performed by Kanze, Kongō and Kita schools
HYAKUMAN (百万) (miscellaneous or demon play)
　　by Komparu Zempō
　　Performed by all schools except Hōshō
IKKAKU SENNIN (一角仙人) (miscellaneous or demon play)
　　by Komparu Zempō
　　Performed by all schools except Hōshō
IKARIZUKI (碇潜) (warrior or miscellaneous play)
　　Author unknown
　　Performed by Kanze and Kongō schools
IKUTA ATSUMORI (生田敦盛) (warrior play)
　　by Komparu Zempō
　　Performed by all schools except Kita
IWAFUNE (岩船) (demon play)
　　Author unknown
IZUTSU (井筒) (woman play)
　　by Zeami
JINEN KOJI (自然居士) (miscellaneous play)
　　by Kannami
KAGEKIYO (景清) (miscellaneous play)
　　Author unknown, but usually attributed to Zeami
KAGETSU (花月) (miscellaneous play)
　　Author unknown, but probably by Zeami
KAKITSUBATA (杜若) (woman play)
　　Probably by Zeami
KAMO (賀茂) (god play)
　　Author unknown, but attributed to Komparu Zenchiku
KAMO MONOGURUI (加茂物狂) (miscellaneous play)
　　by Komparu Zenchiku
　　Performed by Hōshō, Kongō and Kita schools
KANAWA (鉄輪) (miscellaneous play)
　　Author unknown
KANEHIRA (兼平) (warrior play)
　　Attributed to Zeami
KANTAN (邯鄲) (miscellaneous play)
　　Author uncertain, but probably by Zeami
KANYŌKYŪ (咸陽宮) (miscellaneous play)
　　Author unknown
　　Performed by all schools except Komparu
KAPPO (合浦) (demon play)
　　Author unknown
　　Performed by Kanze school only
KASHIWAZAKI (柏崎) (miscellaneous play)
　　by Enami Saemon Gorō
　　Adapted by Zeami
　　Performed by all schools except Kita
KASUGA RYŪJIN (春日竜神) (demon play)
　　Attributed to Zeami
　　Performed by all schools except Kita
KAYOI KOMACHI (通小町) (miscellaneous play)
　　by Kannami
KAZURAGI (葛城) (woman or miscellaneous play)
　　Author unknown, but attributed to Zeami
KAZURAGI TENGU (葛城天狗) (demon play)
　　by Kongō Nagatoshi
　　Performed by Kita school only
KIKUJIDŌ (菊慈童) (miscellaneous play)
　　Author unknown
　　Referred to as *Makurajidō* by schools other than

Kanze

Kɪɴsᴀᴛsᴜ (金札) (demon play)
  by Kannami

Kɪɴᴜᴛᴀ (砧) (miscellaneous play)
  by Zeami

Kɪsᴏ (木曾) (miscellaneous play)
  Author unknown
  Performed by Kanze school only

Kɪʏᴏᴛsᴜɴᴇ (清経) (warrior play)
  by Zeami

Kᴏᴄʜō (胡蝶) (woman play)
  by Kanze Kojirō Nobumitsu
  Performed by all schools except Kita

Kᴏɢō (小督) (miscellaneous play)
  Attributed to Zeami

Kᴏɪ ɴᴏ ᴏᴍᴏɴɪ (恋重荷) (miscellaneous play)
  by Zeami
  Performed by Kanze and Komparu schools only

Kᴏᴋᴀᴊɪ (小鍛治) (demon play)
  Author unknown

Kōᴛᴇɪ (皇帝) (demon play)
  by Kanze Kojirō Nobumitsu
  Performed by all schools except Komparu

Kᴏsᴏᴅᴇ sᴏɢᴀ (小袖曾我) (miscellaneous play)
  Author unknown, but attributed to Miyamasu

Kōᴜ (項羽) (miscellaneous or demon play)
  Attributed to Zeami

Kōʏᴀ ᴍᴏɴᴏɢᴜʀᴜɪ (高野物狂) (miscellaneous play)
  Author unknown
  Performed by all schools except Komparu

Kᴜᴍᴀsᴀᴋᴀ (熊坂) (demon play)
  Author unknown

Kᴜʀᴀᴍᴀ ᴛᴇɴɢᴜ (鞍馬天拘) (demon play)
  by Miyamasu

Kᴜʀᴇʜᴀ (呉服) (god play)
  Attributed to Zeami

Kᴜʀᴏᴢᴜᴋᴀ (黒塚) (demon play)
  Author unknown

Kᴜʀᴜᴍᴀᴢᴏ (車僧) (demon play)
  Attributed to Zeami

Kᴜsᴀɴᴀɢɪ (草薙) (miscellaneous or demon play)
  Author unknown
  Performed by Hōshō school only

Kᴜsᴇɴᴏᴛᴏ (九世戸) (god play)
  by Kanze Kojirō Nobumitsu
  Performed by Kanze school only

Kᴜsᴜ ɴᴏ ᴛsᴜʏᴜ (楠露) (miscellaneous play)
  Author unknown
  Performed by Kanze school only

Kᴜᴢᴜ (国栖) (demon play)
  Author unknown

Mᴀᴋɪɢɪɴᴜ (巻絹) (miscellaneous play)
  Author unknown
  Performed by all schools except Komparu

Mᴀᴋᴜʀᴀᴊɪᴅō (枕慈童) (miscellaneous play)
  Author unknown
  Referred to as *Kikujidō* by schools other than Kanze

Mᴀɴᴊū (満仲) (miscellaneous play)
  Author unknown

Mᴀᴛsᴜᴋᴀᴢᴇ (松風) (woman play)
  by Kannami, adapted by Zeami

Mᴀᴛsᴜᴍᴜsʜɪ (松虫) (miscellaneous play)
  Author unknown

Mᴀᴛsᴜɴᴏ-ᴏ (松尾) (god play)

  Author unknown, but possibly by Zeami
  Performed by Hōshō school only

Mᴀᴛsᴜʏᴀᴍᴀ ᴋᴀɢᴀᴍɪ (松山鏡) (demon play)
  Author unknown, but possibly by Zeami
  Performed by Kanze, Kongō and Kita schools

Mᴀᴛsᴜʏᴀᴍᴀ ᴛᴇɴɢᴜ (松山天拘) (demon play)
  Author unknown
  Performed by Kongō school only

Mᴇᴋᴀʀɪ (和布刈) (god play)
  Author unknown
  Performed by all schools except Komparu

Mɪᴄʜɪᴍᴏʀɪ (通盛) (warrior play)
  Text by Iami, revised by Zeami

Mɪɪᴅᴇʀᴀ (三井寺) (miscellaneous play)
  Author unknown

Mɪᴍᴏsᴜsᴏ (御裳濯) (god play)
  Probably by Zeami
  Performed by Komparu and Kita schools

Mɪɴᴀsᴇ (水無瀬) (miscellaneous play)
  Author unknown
  Performed by Kita school only

Mɪɴᴀᴢᴜᴋɪʙᴀʀᴀɪ (水無月祓) (miscellaneous play)
  by Zeami
  Performed by Kanze school only

Mɪɴᴏʙᴜ (身延) (woman play)
  Author unknown
  Performed by Kanze school only

Mɪᴛsᴜʏᴀᴍᴀ (三山) (miscellaneous play)
  Attributed to Zeami
  Performed by Hōshō and Kongō schools

Mɪᴡᴀ (三輪) (woman or miscellaneous play)
  Author unknown

Mᴏᴄʜɪᴢᴜᴋɪ (望月) (warrior or miscellaneous play)
  Author unknown

Mᴏᴍɪᴊɪɢᴀʀɪ (紅葉狩) (demon play)
  by Kanze Kojirō Nobumitsu

Mᴏʀɪʜɪsᴀ (盛久) (miscellaneous play)
  by Kanze Jūrō Motomasa

Mᴏᴛᴏᴍᴇᴢᴜᴋᴀ (求塚) (miscellaneous play)
  by Kannami
  Performed by all schools except Komparu

Mᴜʀᴏɢɪᴍɪ (室君) (miscellaneous play)
  Author unknown
  Performed by Kanze and Komparu schools

Mᴜᴛsᴜʀᴀ (六浦) (woman play)
  Author unknown

Nᴀᴋᴀᴍɪᴛsᴜ (仲光) (miscellaneous play)
  Author unknown
  Performed by all schools except Komparu. Referred to as *Manjū* by schools other than Kanze

Nᴀɴɪᴡᴀ (難波) (god play)
  by Zeami

Nᴇᴢᴀᴍᴇ (寝覚) (god play)
  Author unknown
  Performed by Kanze school only

Nɪsʜɪᴋɪɢɪ (錦木) (miscellaneous play)
  by Zeami

Nɪsʜɪᴋɪᴅᴏ (錦戸) (miscellaneous play)
  by Miyamasu
  Performed by Kanze and Hōshō schools

Nᴏɴᴏᴍɪʏᴀ (野宮) (woman play)
  Author not certain, but generally ascribed to Zeami

Nᴏᴍᴏʀɪ (野守) (demon play)
  by Zeami

Nᴜᴇ (鵺) (demon play)

by Zeami

OBASUTE (姨捨) (woman play)
by Zeami
Performed by all schools except Komparu

OCHIBA (落葉) (woman play)
Attributed to Zeami
Performed by Kongō and Kita schools

OJIO (小塩) (miscellaneous play)
by Komparu Zenchiku

OHARA GOKŌ (小原御幸) (woman play)
Author unknown, but sometimes attributed to Zeami

OIMATSU (老松) (god play)
by Zeami

OMINAESHI (女郎花) (miscellaneous play)
Author unknown

ŌEYAMA (大江山) (demon play)
by Miyamasu

ŌMU KOMACHI (鸚鵡小町) (woman play)
Attributed to Zeami
Performed by all schools except Komparu

ŌYASHIRO (大社) (god play)
by Kanze Yajirō Nagatoshi
Performed by Kanze, Kongō and Kita schools

OROCHI (大蛇) (miscellaneous or demon play)
by Kanze Kojirō Nobumitsu
Performed by Hōshō, Kongō and Kita schools

RAIDEN (雷電) (demon play)
Author unknown
Performed by all schools except Komparu

RASHŌMON (羅生門) (miscellaneous or demon play)
by Kanze Kojirō Nobumitsu
Performed by all schools except Komparu

RINZŌ (輪蔵) (god or demon play)
by Kanze Yajirō Nagatoshi
Performed by Kanze and Kita schools

RŌDAIKO (籠太鼓)
Attributed to Zeami

RŌGIŌ (籠祇王) (miscellaneous play)
Author unknown
Performed by Kita school only

RYŌKO (竜虎) (demon play)
by Kanze Kojiro Nobumitsu
Performed by Kanze and Kita schools

SAGI (鷺) (woman or miscellaneous play)
Author unknown
Performed by all schools except Komparu

SAIGYŌZAKURA (西行桜) (woman and miscellaneous play)
by Zeami

SAKAHOKO (逆矛) (god play)
Author unknown
Performed by Kanze school only

SAKURAGAWA (桜川) (miscellaneous play)
by Zeami

SANEMORI (実盛) (warrior play)
by Zeami

SANSHŌ (三笑) (miscellaneous play)
Author unknown
Performed by all schools except Komparu

SAOYAMA (佐保山) (god play)
Attributed to Zeami
Performed by Komparu school only

SEIGANJI (誓願寺) (woman play)
Attributed to Zeami

SEIŌBO (西王母) (god play)
Attributed to Zeami

SEKIDERA KOMACHI (関寺小町) (woman or miscellaneous play)
Author uncertain, but probably by Zeami

SEKIHARA YOICHI (関原与一) (warrior or miscellaneous play)
Author unknown
Performed by Kita school only

SEMIMARU (蟬丸) (miscellaneous play)
by Zeami

SENJU (千手) (woman play)
Often attributed to Komparu Zenchiku, but probably by Zeami

SESSHŌSEKI (殺生石) (miscellaneous or demon play)
Author unknown, but possibly by Saami

SETTAI (摂待) (miscellaneous play)
Author unknown
Performed by all schools except Komparu

SHAKKYŌ (石橋) (demon play)
Author unknown

SHARI (舎利) (demon play)
Attributed to Zeami

SHICHIKIOCHI (七騎落) (miscellaneous play)
Author unknown

SHIGA (志賀) (god play)
Attributed to Zeami
Performed by all schools except Komparu

SHIGEMORI (重盛) (miscellaneous play)
Author unknown
Performed by Kita school only

SHIRAHIGE (白髭) (god play)
Attributed to Kannami
Performed by Kanze, Komparu and Kita schools

SHIRONUSHI (代主) (god play)
Author unknown, but possibly by Zeami
Performed by Kanze school only

SHŌJŌ (猩々) (demon play)
Author unknown

SHŌKI (鐘馗) (demon play)
Author unknown

SHŌKUN (昭君) (demon play)
Author unknown, but text may antedate Zeami

SHŌZON (正尊) (miscellaneous play)
by Kanze Yajirō Nagatoshi

SHUNKAN (俊寛) (miscellaneous play)
Author unknown

SHUNNEI (春栄) (miscellaneous play)
by Zeami

SHUNZEI TADANORI (俊成忠度) (warrior play)
by Naitō Kawachi-no-kami
Performed by all schools except Komparu

SŌSHI ARAI KOMACHI (草子洗小町) (woman play)
Author unknown

SOTOBA KOMACHI (卒都婆小町) (miscellaneous play)
by Kannami

SUMA GENJI (須磨源氏) (demon play)
Adapted by Zeami
Performed by all schools except Komparu

SUMIDAGAWA (隅田川) (miscellaneous play)
by Kanze Jūrō Motomasa

SUMIYOSHI-MŌDE (住吉詣) (woman or miscellaneous play)
Author unknown
Performed by Kanze, Kongō and Kita schools

SUMIZOME SAKURA (墨染桜) (woman play)
    Author unknown
    Performed by Kongō school only
TADANOBU (忠信) (miscellaneous play)
    by Komparu Zenchiku .
    Performed by Kanze and Hōshō schools
TADANORI (忠度) (warrior play)
    by Zeami
    Performed by Kanze, Kongō and Kita schools
TAEMA (当麻) (demon play)
    by Zeami
TAIHEI SHŌJŌ (大瓶猩々) (demon play)
    Author unknown
    Performed by Kanze school only
TAIZAN BUKUN (泰山府君) (miscellaneous and demon play)
    by Zeami
    Performed by Kongō school only
TAKASAGO (高砂) (god play)
    by Zeami
TAKENOYUKI (竹雪) (miscellaneous play)
    Attributed to Zeami
    Performed by Hōshō and Kita schools
TAMAKAZURA (玉葛) (miscellaneous play)
    by Komparu Zenchiku
TAMANOI (玉井) (god play)
    by Kanze Kojirō Nobumitsu
    Performed by Kanze, Kongō and Kita schools
TAMURA (田村) (warrior play)
    Attributed to Zeami
TANIKŌ (谷行) (miscellaneous or demon play)
    by Komparu Zenchiku
TATSUTA (竜田) (woman or miscellaneous play)
    Author unknown, but probably by Zeami
    Performed by Kanze school only
TEIKA (定家) (woman play)
    Probably by Komparu Zenchiku
TENKO (天鼓) (miscellaneous play)
    Author unknown
TŌBOKU (東北) (woman play)
    Probably by Zeami
TŌBŌSAKU (東方朔) (god play)
    by Komparu Zempō
    Performed by Kanze, Komparu and Kita schools
TŌEI (藤栄) (warrior or miscellaneous play)
    Author unknown
    Performed by all schools except Kanze
TŌGAN KOJI (東岸居士) (miscellaneous play)
    by Zeami
    Performed by all schools except Komparu
TOKUSA (木賊) (woman and miscellaneous play)
    Probably by Zeami
    Performed by all schools except Komparu
TOMOAKIRA (知章) (warrior play)
    Probably by Zeami
    Performed by all schools except Hōshō
TOMOE (巴) (warrior play)
    Author unknown
TOMONAGA (朝長) (warrior play)
    Probably by Zeami
TORIOIBUNE (鳥追舟) (miscellaneous play)
    Author unknown
TŌRU (融) (demon play)
    by Zeami
TŌSEN (唐船) (miscellaneous play)

by Toyama Matagorō Yoshihiro
TSUCHIGUMO (土蜘蛛) (demon play)
    Author unknown
TSUCHIGURUMA (土車) (miscellaneous play)
    by Zeami
    Performed by Kanze and Kita schools
TSUNEMASA (経政) (warrior play)
    Author unknown
TSURUKAME (鶴亀) (god play)
    Author unknown
UCHITO-MŌDE (内外詣) (god play)
    by Kongō Matabei Nagayori
    Performed by Kongō school only
UGETSU (雨月) (miscellaneous play)
    by Komparu Zenchiku
UKAI (鵜飼) (demon play)
    by Enami Saemon Gorō; adapted by Zeami
UKIFUNE (浮舟) (miscellaneous play)
    Text by Yokoo Motohisa; music by Zeami
    Performed by all schools except Hōshō
UKON (右近) (god play)
    by Zeami (minor adaptation by Kanze Kojirō)
    Performed by Kanze, Hōshō and Kongō schools
UME (梅) (woman play)
    by Kamo no Mabuchi (?)
    Performed by Kanze school only
UMEGAE (梅枝) (miscellaneous play)
    Attributed to Zeami
UNEME (采女) (woman play)
    by Zeami
UNOMATSURI (鵜祭) (god play)
    Author unknown
    Performed by Komparu school only
UNRININ (雲林院) (miscellaneous play)
    Author unknown. Text in Zeami's hand survives
    Performed by all schools except Komparu
UROKOGATA (鱗形) (god play)
    Author unknown
    Performed by Kongō and Kita schools
UTAURA (歌占) (miscellaneous play)
    by Kanze Jūrō Motomasa
UTŌ (善知鳥) (miscellaneous play)
    Author unknown
YAMAHIME (山姫) (woman play)
    Author unknown
    Performed by Kita school
YAMAUBA (山姥) (demon play)
    Author uncertain, but probably by Zeami
YASHIMA (八島) (warrior play)
    Author uncertain, but probably by Zeami
YORIMASA (頼政) (warrior play)
    by Zeami
YOROBOSHI (弱法師) (miscellaneous play)
    by Kanze Jūrō Motomasa
YŌRŌ (養老) (god play)
    by Zeami
YOSHINO SHIZUKA (吉野静) (woman or miscellaneous play)
    by Kannami
YOSHINO TENJIN (吉野天人) (woman play)
    by Kanze Kojirō Nobumitsu
    Performed by Kanze school only
YOUCHI SOGA (夜討曾我) (miscellaneous play)
    by Miyamasu
YŌKIHI (楊貴妃) (woman play)

by Komparu Zenchiku

Yūgao (夕顔) (woman play)
　　by Zeami
　　Performed by Kanze, Kongō and Kita schools
Yugyō yanagi (遊行柳) (woman or miscellaneous play)
　　by Kanze Kojirō Nobumitsu
Yuki (雪) (woman play)
　　Author unknown
　　Performed by Kongō school only
Yumi yawata (弓八幡) (god play)
　　by Zeami

Yuya (熊野) (woman play)
　　Author unknown, but generally attributed to Zeami
Zegai (善界) (demon play)
　　by Takeda Hōin Munemori
Zenji soga (禅師曾我) (miscellaneous play)
　　Author unknown
　　Performed by Kanze, Hōshō and Kita schools

Note. The authorship of the plays has yet to be established firmly. The above attributions reflect current scholarship in Japan.

BIBLIOGRAPHY ·

Note: With two exceptions, the following list is confined to books.

Translations and Studies in Western Languages

Araki, James T. *The Ballad-Drama of Medieval Japan*. Berkeley, 1964.

Fenollosa, Ernest, and Pound, Ezra. *The Classic Noh Theatre of Japan*., New York, 1959.

Keene, Donald (ed.) *Twenty Plays of the Nō Theatre*. New York, 1970.

Komiya, Toyotaka. *Japanese Music and Drama in the Meiji Era*, Tokyo, 1956.

Nippon Gakujutsu Shinkōkai. *Japanese Noh Drama*. 3 vols. Tokyo, 1955–60.

O'Neill, P.G. *Early Nō Drama*, London, 1958.

Peri, Noël. *Le Nô*. Tokio, 1944.

Renondeau, Gaston. *Nô*, Tokio, 1954.

Sakanishi, Shio. *Kyōgen: Comic Interludes of Japan*, Boston, 1938. (Reprinted as *The Ink-Smeared Lady and Other Kyōgen*, Tokyo, 1960).

Sieffert, René. *La Tradition Secrète du Nô*, Paris, 1960. (A translation of critical writings by Zeami, and of a program of Nō and Kyōgen plays.)

Ueda, Makoto. *The Old Pine Tree and Other Noh Plays*, Lincoln, 1962.

Waley, Arthur. *The Nō Plays of Japan*. London, 1921.

Texts of Nō and Kyōgen

Koyama, Hiroshi 小山弘志. *Kyōgen Shū* 狂言集. *Nihon Koten Bungaku Taikei* series. 2 vols. 1960–61. Texts of the Ōkura school in modern orthography. The notes consist mainly of quotations from the 1603 Japanese-Portuguese dictionary.

Nonomura, Kaizō 野々村成三 and Furukawa Hisashi 古川久. *Kyōgen Shū. Nihon Koten Zensho* series. 3 vols. 1953–56. An excellent edition of texts of the now defunct Sagi school of Kyōgen.

Nonomura, Kaizō. *Yōkyoku Sambyakugojūban Shū. Nihon Meicho Zenshū* series. 1928. Valuable for the texts of plays no longer in the repertory.

Ōwada, Tateki 大和田建樹 *Yōkyoku Hyōshaku*. 1907. Outdated in most respects, this volume is still useful for texts not easily found elsewhere.

Sanari, Kentarō 佐成謙太郎. *Yōkyoku Taikan* 謡曲大観. 7 vols. 2nd ed. 1954. An indispensable work. Gives texts with modern language translations.

Sasano, Ken 笹野堅. *Nō Kyōgen*. 3 vols. *Iwanami Bunko* series. 2nd ed., 1956. Texts of the Ōkura school. A lengthy introduction but no notes.

Tanaka, Mitsuru 田中充. *Bangai Yōkyoku. Koten Bunko* series. 1950. Texts of plays not in current repertory. No notes.

Tanaka, Mitsuru. *Yōkyoku Shū. Nihon Koten Zensho* series. 3 vols. 1949–57. Notes, exceedingly scarce in the first volume, are generous by the third. Gives Kurumaya texts, the basic ones of Komparu school.

Yokomichi, Mario 横道萬里雄 and Omote, Akira 表章. *Yōkyoku Shū. Nihon Koten Bungaku Taikei* series. 1963. Excellent annotated texts, but a rigid criterion of authorship results in some masterpieces by unidentified writers being omitted or given far less attention than poor works by identified writers.

General Works

Engeki Hyakka Daijiten 演劇百科大辞典. 6 vols. 1961. An invaluable encyclopedia of the theatre.

Furukawa, Hisashi. *Nō no Sekai*. 1960. An unpretentious but excellent introduction.

Hayashiya, Tatsusaburō 林屋辰三郎. *Kabuki Izen*. 1954. A study of Japanese theatre and its social background before the rise of Kabuki.

Kobayashi, Shizuo 小林静雄. *Nōgakushi Kenkyū*. 1945. A scholarly and well-documented study of the history of Nō, especially during the Muromachi period.

Kongō, Iwao 金剛巌. *Nō*. 1948. Much of the material is elementary, but the book is dotted with observations worthy of a master actor.

Maruoka, Akira 丸岡明. *Nihon no Nō*. 1957. Interesting descriptions of performances since the war.

Miyake, Noboru 三宅襄. *Nō*. 1948. Excellent general study.

Nishio, Minoru 西尾実 and others. *Yōkyoku Kyōgen*. 1961. Extremely valuable for its surveys of studies in different aspects of Nō and Kyōgen, and for its reproduction of various important historical and critical texts.

Nogami, Toyoichirō 野上豊一郎. *Nō: Kenkyū to Hakken*. 1930. A pioneer work of scholarship, containing stimulating essays.

Nogami, Toyoichirō (ed.) *Nōgaku Zensho.* 6 vols. 1942–44. Indispensable collection of essays on all aspects of Nō and Kyōgen. The 1952–58 revision in five volumes is inferior.

Nose, Asaji 能勢朝次. *Nōgaku Genryū Kō.* 1938. The basic study of the development of Nō. A masterpiece.

Nose, Asaji. *Nōgaku Kenkyū.* 1940. Excellent essays on various topics.

Yokoi, Haruno 横井春野. *Nōgaku Zenshi.* 1917. Extremely detailed for Tokugawa period. Not to be consulted lightly.

Yokomichi, Mario and Masuda, Shōzō 増田正造. *Nō to Kyōgen.* 1959. Basic information on Nō and Kyōgen.

Ikeuchi, Nobuyoshi 池内信嘉. *Nōgaku Seisuiki.* 2 vols. 1925–6. A massive compilation of materials on Nō during the Tokugawa and Meiji eras.

Biographical

Kobayashi, Shizuo. *Zeami* 世阿弥. 1958. A brilliant study of Zeami's life, art, plays, and critical works.

Kobayashi, Shizuo. *Yōkyoku Sakusha no Kenkyū.* 1941. Biographies of the principal Nō dramatists. A careful study.

Kōzai, Tsutomu 香西精. *Zeami Shinkō.* 1962. Important essays on Zeami's life, religious beliefs, and style.

Nogami, Toyoichirō. *Kannami Kiyotsugu* 観阿弥清次. 1949. Stretches out to 155 pages a meagre number of facts.

Nogami, Toyoichirō. *Zeami Motokiyo.* 1938. A useful study of Zeami and his art.

Usui, Nobuyoshi 臼井信義. *Ashikaga Yoshimitsu* 足利義満. *Jimbutsu Sōsho* series. 1960. A useful biography of Zeami's great patron.

Nō Criticism

Kawase, Kazuma 川瀬一馬. *Gendaigoyaku Kadensho.* 1962. A translation into modern Japanese of Zeami's most famous work.

Konishi, Jinichi 小西甚一. *Nōgakuron Kenkyū.* 1961. Brilliant essays on the theories of Zeami and later dramatists.

Konishi, Jinichi. *Zeami Jūrokubu Shū.* 1954. A translation into modern Japanese of important treatises by Zeami.

Nishio, Minoru (ed.). *Karon Shū; Nōgakuron Shū. Nihon Koten Bungaku Taikei* series. 1961. Excellent edition with ample notes of Zeami's writings.

Nose, Asaji. *Zeami Jūrokubu Shū Hyōshaku.* 2 vols. 1944. Indispensable translation of and commentary on Zeami's writings.

Omote, Akira (ed.) *Bushō Goma* 舞正語磨. 1958. Text of the seventeenth-century attack on the Kita school, with an introduction.

Masks

Gotō, Hajime 後藤淑. *Nōmenshi Kenkyū Josetsu.* 1964. An important study of masks preserved at various remote shrines and temples. Provides a means of understanding the later masks.

Kaneko, Ryōun 金子良運. *Kamen no Bi.* 1961. A well-

illustrated introduction to all varieties of masks in Japan, with helpful pointers for identifying them.

Kongō, Iwao. *Nō to Nōmen.* 1951. A great actor's personal view of the beauty of the masks.

Nogami, Toyoichirō. *Nōmen Ronkō.* 1944. A comprehensive treatment of the masks.

Noma, Seiroku 野間清六. *Nihon Kamen Shi.* 1943. Good especially for pre-Nō masks.

Shirasu, Masako 白洲正子. *Nōmen.* 1964. Fine photographs and a sensitive appreciation of the masks.

Costumes

Fujishiro, Tsugio 藤城継夫. *Shashin de Miru Nō no Funsō.* 1962. A most useful guide to Nō costumes.

Noma, Seiroku. *Kosode to Nō Ishō.* 1965. Lovely reproductions of Nō and Kyōgen robes, but the text is insufficiently informative.

The Actors

Nogami, Toyoichirō. (ed.) *Yōkyoku Geijutsu.* 1936. In addition to the general discussion by the editor, the book contains accounts by outstanding actors of their interpretations of different genres of Nō.

Sakurama, Kyūsen 桜間弓川. *Sakurama Geiwa.* 1948. A small volume of recollections and observations by a great actor.

Shigeyama, Sensaku 茂山千作. *Kyōgen Hachijūnen.* 1951. Reminiscences of the famous Kyōgen actor.

Shirasu, Masako. *Umewaka Minoru Kikigaki* 梅若実聞書. 1951. The story, in a transcription of his own words, of the son of the great Meiji actor, a self-effacing artist who never achieved the highest fame.

Yanagizawa, Hideki 柳沢英樹. *Hōshō Kurō Den* 宝生九郎傳. 1944. Ostensibly a biography of the great actor of the Meiji era, it hardly attempts to penetrate surface facts; valuable instead for its account of Nō during a critical period.

Regional Entertainments

Honda, Yasuji 本田安次. *Minzoku Geinō* 民族芸能. 1962. Brief descriptions with photographs of many regional entertainments.

Honda, Yasuji. *Nō oyobi Kyōgen Kō.* 1943. Miscellaneous essays in which the author attempts to discover early forms of Nō and Kyōgen in surviving rural theatricals.

Honda, Yasuji. *Okina sono hoka.* 1958. Intended as a continuation of the preceding title, it describes in addition to *Okina* various old forms of Nō and Kyōgen surviving today, including Mibu Kyōgen.

Ikeda, Yasaburō 池田弥三郎. *Nihon Geinō Denshō Ron.* 1962. Essays on the folkloristic and social background of the Japanese arts and their transmission. Popularly written.

Takeuchi, Katsutarō 竹内勝太郎. *Geijutsu Minzokugaku Kenkyū.* 1949. Includes essays on the beginnings of Nō and on Mibu Kyōgen.

Toita, Michizō 戸井田道三. *Nō: Kami to Kojiki no Geijutsu.* 1964. An interesting approach to Nō from a folkloristic and anthropological viewpoint.

Performance of Nō and Kyōgen

Araki, Yoshio 荒木良雄 and Shigeyama Sennojō 茂山千之丞. *Kyōgen*. 1956. The historical appreciation of Kyōgen by Araki is followed by Shigeyama's elucidation of the techniques of performance.

Kobayashi, Shizuo. *Yōkyoku no Kanshō*. 1939. Though intended primarily for high-school students, the book is important because of its discussion of how the plays considered are performed.

Miyake, Noboru. *Nō Enshutsu no Kenkyū*. 1948. The most detailed explanations of the *kogaki* and other aspects of performance.

Suda, Atsuo 須田敦夫. *Nihon Gekijō Shi no Kenkyū*. 1957. Devoted in part to a study of the Nō stage.

Music

Kikkawa, Eiji 吉川英史. *Nihon Ongaku no Rekishi*. 1965. An impressive study of all aspects of Japanese music.

Minagawa, Tatsuo 皆川達夫. "Japanese Noh Music" in *Journal of the American Musicological Society*, Vol. X, No. 3, 1957.

Yokomichi, Mario. "Nō no Ongaku" in booklet accompanying records of Nō produced in 1963 for the six hundredth anniversary of Zeami's birth.

INDEX

actors and acting, 15, 16, 17, 23–26, 27, 32–33, 34, 39–40, 42, 43, 57–59; training of actors, 57–59

Adachigahara, 59; see also *Kurozuka*

ado (Kyōgen role), 56

aesthetic appeal of Nō, 17

ageuta (Nō song), 49

ai (interlude), 21, 49, 55

ai-kyōgen (interval recitations), 21, 54, 55

ai-kyōgen actor, 21, 55

Akechi-uchi, 38

amateurs and amateur performances, 16, 37, 38, 45, 67; *see also* regional performances of Nō and Kyōgen

Aoi no Ue, 38, 51, 53, 63, 71

Aoyama Palace, Nō stage at, 43

Ariwara no Narihira, 52, 73, 87

Ashikaga Yoshihisa, 37

Ashikaga Yoshimasa, 37, 65, 66, 75

Ashikaga Yoshimitsu, 23, 31, 32, 33–34, 36, 37, 42, 43

Ashikaga Yoshimochi, 33, 34

Ashikaga Yoshinori, 31, 34, 35, 36

Ataka, 22, 53, 62

atoza (rear section of stage), 19, 75, 77

Atsumori (*Atsumori*), 50–51

Atsumori, 20, 26, 46, 50

audience, character of, 14, 16–17, 42, 73; seating of, 19, 75

audience appeal of Nō, 14–15, 16; of Kyōgen, 27, 56

ballet, Nō dance contrasted with, 71, 73

Bashō ("The Plantain Tree"), 65

bass drum, see *taiko*

benefit performances (*kanjin* Nō), 34, 35, 39, 40–41, 42

Benkei: in *Ataka,* 62; in *Funa Benkei,* 54, 75; in *Kanjinchō,* 53; in *Shōzon,* 54

"Benkei in the Boat," see *Funa Benkei*

Bernhardt, Sarah, 24

beshimi mask, 64

Biblical themes in Nō, 39

Bishamon, 64

Bishamon mask, 64

"Blind Man Looks at the Moon, The," see *Tsukimi Zatō*

"Book of Nō Composition, The," see *Nōsakusho*

"Book of the Transmission of the Flower, The," see *Kadensho*

"Book of the Way of the Highest Flower, The," see *Shikadōsho*

Buddhist elements in Nō, 17, 28–29, 36, 48

bugaku, 29, 39, 63, 75

bugaku masks, 63

Bunraku, 39, 41

Bushō Goma, 25

categories of Kyōgen, 26

categories of Nō, 21–22

categories of roles, 20–21

Central Asia, dance of, 29

character types in Nō, 23; in Kyōgen, 26

Chikatō, 54

child actors, 21, 32, 56, 57

child roles, see *kokata*

"chill," see *hie*

China, 14, 29, 31, 38, 78; Japanese relations with, 31, 38; theatre of, 14, 29

Chinese immigrants in Japan, 26

Chinese influences on Japanese dance, 29

Chinese personages in Nō, 38, 54, 77

chōken robe, 66

choreography, *see* dance as element of Nō

chorus, 19, 20, 21, 39, 67, 68

Chōryō, 37

chūjō mask, 61

chūkei fan, 78

chūnomai (Nō dance), 72, 73

chū-nori rhythm, 68

Chūsonji, Nō performances at, 92

climax, see *kyū*

color in costumes, 65–66

comedy, *see* Kyōgen

comic origins of Nō, 13–14

commedia dell'arte, 26

"companion," see *tsure*

Confucian ethics of Tokugawa shogunate, 39

Hōshō school of Nō, 30, 37, 39, 42, 44, 59, 60, 69, 78; scene from performances by, 87
Hōshō Yagorō, 42

Ichijō Kanera, 36
Ichinotani, battle of, 50
iemoto system, 58–59
Ieyasu, *see* Tokugawa Ieyasu
Ikkyū, 36
Imakumano Shrine, Nō performances at, 31, 32
"imitation of things," see *monomane*
"Imperial Warship," see *Miikusabune*
India, dances of, 25; music of, 29
Inland Sea, 19, 31, 75
innovations in modern Nō theatre, 76
inori (Nō dance), 73
interlude, see *ai*
interpretation of roles, 15, 16
introduction of Nō play, see *jo*
Inuō, *see* Dōami
"Iris, The," see *Kakitsubata*
iro, *see* color in costumes
iroe (Nō dance), 73
Ise Monogatari, 18
Ise Shrine, *see* Great Shrine of Ise
Ishigami, 56
Ishikawa Tatsuemon (mask-maker), 64, 96
issei (entrance song), 48, 68
Itsukushima Shrine, Nō performances at, 92; Nō stage at, 19, 75–76
Iwakura Tomomi, 43, 44, 58
Iwasaki Yanosuke, 76
Izumi school of Kyōgen, 41, 55, 60, 78; scene from performances by, 90
Izutsu, 23, 52, 77, 87

jars under Nō stage, 19, 76
Jinen Koji (*Jinen Koji*), 53
Jinen Koji, 32, 53
jo (introduction of Nō play), 21, 29, 48, 72
Jones, Stanleigh H., Jr., 51
jonomai (Nō dance), 73

Kabuki, 22, 37, 39, 43, 44, 53, 59
Kadensho ("The Book of the Transmission of the Flower"), 33
kagami-ita ("mirror boards"), 13
Kagekiyo (*Kagekiyo*), 69, 77, 89
Kagekiyo, 54, 69, 77, 89
Kagura (Shinto dances), 14
kagura (Nō dance), 72
Kagyū, 90
kakegoe (cry), 70
kakekotoba (pivot word), 46–47
kakeri (Nō dance), 73
Kakitsubata ("The Iris"), 16

kamigakari (style of Kyoto), 37
kamimai (Nō dance), 72, 73
kammuri (head ornament), 65
Kanawa, 73
Kanehira, 51
Kanjinchō, 22, 53
kanjin Nō, *see* benefit performances
Kannami, 25, 30, 31–32, 33, 36, 39; plays of, 32
Kantan, 54
Kanze Motomasa, 69
Kanze Sakon, 68–69
Kanze school of Nō, 30, 37, 39, 42, 44, 59, 60, 61, 78; scenes from performances by, 83, 87, 89
kashira wig, 65
Kasuga Festival, 37
Kasuga Shrine, Nō performances at, 13, 28, 75
Kasui, 54
kata (gestures), 16, 17, 72
Kayoi Komachi, 32
Kazumō, 64
kazuramono, *see* woman plays
Kintōsho, 35
Kinuta, 47–48, 53, 65
kiriago ("split jaw") mask, 93
kirido (door for chorus), 19, 20
kiri Nō, *see* demon plays
Kirokuda ("Six Loads of Lumber"), 91
Kita Roppeita, 23, 44, 59, 71, 76
Kita school of Nō, 39–40, 44, 59, 60, 78; scenes from performances by, 83, 85, 92
Kita Shichidayū, 46
Kiyohime (*Dōjōji*), 63–64
Kiyotsune, 26, 61
kobeshimi mask, 64
Kōfukuji Temple, Nō and *ennen* performances at, 28–29
kogaki variations, 60
Koi no Omoni, 45
Kojirō Nobumitsu, plays of, 36–37
kokata (child roles), 20, 21, 57, 66
kōken (understudy), 20
Kokinshū, 46
kokushikijō mask, 62, 93
Komachi: in *Kayoi Komachi*, 32; in *Sekidera Komachi*, 95; in *Sotoba Komachi*, 32, 87, 95
Kombu Uri ("The Seaweed Peddler"), 41
Kōmei, Emperor, 43
Komparu school of Nō, 13, 21, 37, 39, 44, 59, 60, 61, 69, 78
Komparu Shirōjirō, 27
Komparu Zempō, plays of, 37, 54
Komparu Zenchiku, 33, 35, 36, 37, 65; plays and critical writings of, 36
Kongō Iwao (former), 44, 60, 62, 71; (present), 66
Kongō Magojirō (mask-maker and actor), 64